BLACKS

CIV

PRACTICE

BLACKSTONE'S

CIVIL PRACTICE

2009

UPDATING SUPPLEMENT

EDITOR-IN-CHIEF

THE RT HON LORD JUSTICE MAURICE KAY

EDITORS

STUART SIME

DEREK FRENCH

CONTRIBUTORS

EVAN ASHFIELD, JULIE BRANNAN
STUART BRIDGE, JULIE BROWNE, IAIN COLVILLE
PETER JOLLY, ADRIAN KEANE, LISA LAURENTI
ANDREW LIDBETTER, ALAN OWENS
WILLIAM ROSE, JOHN UNGLEY, MICHAEL WALKER
MATTHEW WEINIGER, IVOR WEINTROUB
ANGELA WRIGHT

OXFORD
UNIVERSITY PRESS

OXFORD
UNIVERSITY PRESS

Great Clarendon Street, Oxford OX2 6DP

Oxford University Press is a department of the University of Oxford.
It furthers the University's objective of excellence in research, scholarship,
and education by publishing worldwide in

Oxford New York

Auckland Cape Town Dar es Salaam Hong Kong Karachi
Kuala Lumpur Madrid Melbourne Mexico City Nairobi
New Delhi Shanghai Taipei Toronto

With offices in

Argentina Austria Brazil Chile Czech Republic France Greece
Guatemala Hungary Italy Japan Poland Portugal Singapore
South Korea Switzerland Thailand Turkey Ukraine Vietnam

Oxford is a registered trade mark of Oxford University Press
in the UK and in certain other countries

Published in the United States
by Oxford University Press Inc., New York

© Oxford University Press 2008

The moral rights of the authors have been asserted

Database right Oxford University Press (maker)

Crown copyright material is reproduced under Class Licence
Number C01P0000148 with the permission of the Controller of OPSI
and the Queen's Printer for Scotland

First published 2008

British Library Cataloguing in Publication Data
Data available

Library of Congress Cataloging in Publication Data
Data available

Typeset by RefineCatch Ltd, Bungay, Suffolk
Printed in Great Britain
on acid-free paper by
Ashford Colour Press Ltd, Gosport, Hampshire

ISBN 978–0–19–955843–8

1 3 5 7 9 10 8 6 4 2

Introduction

This supplement updates *Blackstone's Civil Practice 2009* and follows the headings and the paragraph numbering used in that edition. This supplement was completed on 5 September 2008. Unless otherwise stated, all changes to legislation, rules, practice directions and court fees considered in this supplement came into force on 1 October 2008.

Please visit the *Blackstone's Civil Practice 2009* companion website at <www.oup.com/ blackstones/civil>, where this supplement is also available.

Contents

Table of Cases

Table of Primary Legislation

Table of Secondary Legislation

Practice Directions

European Secondary Legislation

Supplement to Chapters 1–100

Chapter 1   The Overriding Objective and Sources of Procedural Law

THE CIVIL PROCEDURE RULES 1998

May, must and should

A number of provisions using the words 'should' and 'shall' were changed by the Civil **1.16**
Procedure (Amendment) Rules 2008 (SI 2008/2178) and CPR Update 47, with effect from
1 October 2008. These include r. 3.7(4)(ii), where 'shall' was changed to 'must'; PD 25B,
para. 4.2, where 'should' was changed to 'must', and r. 3.7(6)(b) and 3.7(7) where 'shall' was
changed to 'will'. The intention is to make it clear that the consequence or requirement is
mandatory.

APPLICATION OF THE OVERRIDING OBJECTIVE

Dealing with cases justly

Ultimately the function of the court is to resolve issues between the parties. It does not have **1.27**
the power to dismiss a claim simply on the ground that the claim (or the issue left in a claim)
has a relatively trivial value which will inevitably be exceeded by the costs (*Devaraja v Roy* [2008]
EWHC 464 (QB), LTL 3/6/2008).

Albon v Naza Motor Trading Sdn Bhd [2007] EWHC 2613 (Ch) is reported as *Albon v Naza Motor
Trading Sdn Bhd (No. 5)* at [2008] 1 All ER 995. In *Gilbart v Thomas Graham* [2008] EWCA Civ 897,
LTL 24/6/2008, the Court of Appeal overturned a decision to refuse an adjournment of the trial
date in order to give effect to the overriding objective. The application had been made 21 days
before the date for the trial, which was an unrealistically short time for the defendant (who
had applied for the adjournment) to obtain specific disclosure from the claimant and to
instruct an expert on a loss of profits claim. In *Ratiopharm (UK) Ltd v Alza Corporation* [2008]
EWHC 1182 (Ch), LTL 1/5/2008, six months was regarded as enough time to prepare a patent
infringement claim for trial. The party seeking to avoid the trial date in this case had received
a letter with the allegations in the litigation 13 months before the trial date, so should have
been able to prepare for trial.

Firmer case management control was called for where litigation had taken longer than might
otherwise have been hoped for, and where there was a danger that costs would become
disproportionate (*Multiplex Construction (UK) Ltd v Cleveland Bridge UK Ltd* [2008] EWHC 231 (TCC),
LTL 9/5/2008).

As might be expected, making a fraudulent claim is a serious breach of the overriding
objective (*Ul-Haq v Shah* [2008] EWHC 1896 (QB), LTL 11/8/2008).

Proportionality and costs

It may be appropriate for a defendant to file and serve a single defence to two related claims in **1.29**
order to save costs (*Rosenberg v Nazarov* [2008] EWHC 812 (Ch), LTL 10/4/2008).

Proportionality: examples

Setting aside an order granting permission to serve outside the jurisdiction on the ground that **1.30**
the claim form and witness statement were not signed was regarded as disproportionate in

Colliers International Property Consultants v Colliers Jordan Lee Jafaar Sdn Bhd [2008] EWHC 1524 (Comm), LTL 10/7/2008.

Equal footing

1.31   The tests on striking out and summary judgment remain unchanged even where one party is suffering from an inequality of arms (*Bank of Tokyo-Mitsubishi UFJ Ltd v Baskan Gida Sanayi ve Pazarlama AS* [2008] EWHC 659 (Ch), LTL 17/4/2008).

Chapter 6   Conditional Fee Agreements

ENTERING INTO A CFA

Normal CFAs

6.6   If a normal CFA was entered into before 1 November 2005, the Conditional Fee Agreements Regulations 2000 (SI 2000/692) required the legal representative to state whether he had any interest in any (particularly ATE) insurance he recommended or considered appropriate (reg. 4(2)). Paragraphs (c), (d) and (e) of reg. 4(2) apply cumulatively, and whether or not insurance is in place. A solicitor does have an interest in litigation insurance which is available only to clients of solicitors within a claims management company's scheme. There will be a breach of reg. 4(2)(e) in a normal, pre-1 November 2005, CFA if in such a case the solicitor stated it had no interest in recommending such insurance (*Jones v Wrexham Borough Council* [2007] EWCA Civ 1356, [2008] 1 WLR 1590).

Non-indemnity CFAs

6.7   A non-indemnity CFA is also known as a 'CFA Lite'.

When deciding whether a CFA comes within the Conditional Fee Agreements Regulations 2000 (SI 2000/692), reg. 3A, the court can take into account the whole of the contractual package (the CFA, client care letter and ATE insurance policy). It is not restricted to looking only at the CFA (*Jones v Wrexham Borough Council* [2007] EWCA Civ 1356, [2008] 1 WLR 1590). The court must consider whether the requirements of reg. 3A were met when the agreement was entered into. If at that time there was valid insurance covering the costs and disbursements, the 'or otherwise' requirement in reg. 3A(1) will be satisfied. Possible subsequent avoidance of the insurance is irrelevant (*Jones v Wrexham Borough Council*).

Failure to comply with the Regulations

6.10   **Materially adverse effect**   *Garrett v Halton Borough Council* [2006] EWCA Civ 1017 is also reported at [2007] 1 WLR 554. Comments in the case at [69] to [78] to the effect that what steps a solicitor should reasonably take to discharge the obligation under the Conditional Fee Agreements Regulations 2000 (SI 2000/692), reg. 4(2)(c), depends on the circumstances of the case, were applied in *Wooley v Haden Building Services Ltd* (2008) LTL 18/3/2008 (SCCO). The guidance laid down in *Sarwar v Alam* [2001] EWCA Civ 1401, [2002] 1 WLR 125, only applies in smaller cases, and does not apply to complex claims such as those for work-related mesothelioma.

A denial by the solicitor of having an interest in recommending ATE insurance in breach of the Conditional Fee Agreements Regulations 2000 (SI 2000/692), reg. 4(2)(e), would render the CFA unenforceable (*Jones v Wrexham Borough Council* [2007] EWCA Civ 1356, [2008] 1 WLR 1590).

Staged success fees

There is no need to make a separate assessment of the risk relating to the possible need for a **6.16** detailed assessment of costs when entering into a CFA. The costs of assessment will, in the (probable) absence of a separate success fee, be dealt with in the same way as other base costs in the case (*Crane v Canons Leisure Centre* [2007] EWCA Civ 1352, [2008] 2 All ER 931).

NOTIFICATION OF FUNDING ARRANGEMENT

In PD 43–48, para. 19.2(4), the seven days runs from the date the ATE policy is issued, **6.17** rather than from the date it comes into effect (*Supperstone v Hurst* [2008] EWHC 735 (Ch), LTL 23/4/2008). If a party fails to proffer an adequate explanation for a failure to serve a notice of funding in accordance with CPR, r. 44.15, or if the paying party suffers prejudice as a result of the breach, relief from sanctions will usually be refused (*Supperstone v Hurst*). Provided adequate informal notice is given that relief from sanctions will be sought, the court may entertain an application for relief from sanctions without an application notice or witness statement in support of the application, and it is for the paying party to adduce evidence of any alleged prejudice, not for the party seeking relief to deny prejudice.

ASSESSMENT OF CFA COSTS

Assessment of basic costs

Assessment of basic costs between the parties is usually on the standard basis unless an **6.19** indemnity basis costs order has been made. The standard-form CFA Conditions published by the Law Society define the basic charges as 'our charges for the legal work we do on your claim for damages'. This is wide enough to cover generic work done for clients on claims covered, or intended to be covered, by a GLO, and there is no need for any collateral agreement between the solicitor and client for such generic costs (*Brown v Russell Young and Co.* [2007] EWCA Civ 43, [2008] 1 WLR 525).

In *Crane v Canons Leisure Centre* [2007] EWCA Civ 1352, [2008] 2 All ER 931, a collective CFA defined base costs as 'charges for work done by or on behalf of the Solicitors which would have been payable if this agreement did not provide for a success fee, calculated on the basis of the fees allowable for that work in the court in which the [claim] in question is conducted or would be conducted if proceedings were to be issued'. The costs of the detailed assessment, which was actually conducted by costs consultants engaged by the solicitors, were held to be part of the solicitors' base costs, and to attract the success fee on the same footing as the base costs on the substantive claim.

Chapter 7   Community Legal Service

LEVELS OF SERVICE

Introduction

The schedule to the Community Legal Service (Funding) Order 2007 (SI 2007/2441) sets **7.2** out remuneration rates payable for funded services. A new schedule has been substituted by the Community Legal Service (Funding) (Amendment) Order 2008 (SI 2008/1328). The new schedule applies to matters begun on or after 1 July 2008.

Chapter 8   Pre-action Protocols

PURPOSE OF PRE-ACTION PROTOCOLS

8.1   If a dispute is settled through use of a pre-action protocol, the usual expectation is that the defendant will pay the claimant's reasonable costs assessed, if not agreed, on the basis of the case management track which would have been appropriate for the claim had proceedings been issued (*Birmingham City Council v Lee* [2008] EWCA Civ 891, LTL 30/7/2008).

EXPECTATION OF COMPLIANCE WITH THE PROTOCOLS

8.2   The protocols apply to additional claims under CPR, Part 20, as well as to normal claims under Part 7 (*Daejan Investments Ltd v Park West Club Ltd* [2003] EWHC 2872 (TCC), [2004] BLR 223). However, a pragmatic approach is taken, with due leeway being given to the parties bearing in mind that directions may have been given in the main claim fixing the trial date or window (*Orange Personal Communications Services Ltd v Hoare Lea* [2008] EWHC 223 (TCC), LTL 19/2/2008).

A failure to send a letter of claim was taken into account in *Zambia v Meer Care and Desai* [2008] EWCA Civ 754, LTL 9/7/2008, on an application to set aside judgment for non-attendance under CPR, r. 39.3 (see **60.2** in this supplement).

Whether a sanction should be imposed

8.3   Sanctions, whether in costs or otherwise, should not be imposed where there has been substantial compliance with the relevant protocol (*T. J. Brent Ltd v Black and Veatch Consulting Ltd* [2008] EWHC 1497 (TCC), LTL 3/7/2008).

CONSTRUCTION AND ENGINEERING DISPUTES PROTOCOL

8.45   The Pre-action Protocol for Construction and Engineering Disputes applies to additional claims under CPR, Part 20 (*Daejan Investments Ltd v Park West Club Ltd* [2003] EWHC 2872 (TCC), [2004] BLR 223), although a pragmatic approach has to be taken as there will often be limited time in which to comply with the protocol, issue the claim and get the case ready for any trial (*Alfred McAlpine Capital Projects Ltd v SIAC (UK) Ltd* [2005] EWHC 3139 (TCC), [2006] BLR 139). Care should be taken before granting a stay to enable full compliance with the protocol if that will mean breaking trial directions given in the main proceedings (*Orange Personal Communications Services Ltd v Hoare Lea* [2008] EWHC 223 (TCC), LTL 19/2/2008).

Requirements of the Construction and Engineering Disputes Protocol

8.46   The letter of claim must set out the facts on which the claim is based, identifying the principal contractual terms and statutory provisions relied upon, and the relief sought. It does not have to identify every detail, or the exact amount claimed (*T. J. Brent Ltd v Black and Veatch Consulting Ltd* [2008] EWHC 1497 (TCC), LTL 3/7/2008).

HOUSING DISREPAIR PROTOCOL

8.57   A tenant with a justifiable claim for disrepair which is settled as a result of using the Pre-action Protocol for Housing Disrepair Cases is entitled (subject to the usual discretionary factors on costs) to an order that the landlord pays the tenant's reasonable costs calculated according to the track which the claim would have been allocated to if litigation had been started (para. 3.7; guidance note 4.10 as interpreted by *Birmingham City Council v Lee* [2008] EWCA Civ 891, LTL 30/7/2008). The appropriate order to make is one for costs on the [fast] track basis up to the date the repair work was done (*Birmingham City Council v Lee*).

Chapter 9   Notices before Action

ROAD TRAFFIC CASES

Untraced drivers

Byrne v Motor Insurers Bureau [2007] EWHC 1268 (QB), [2008] 2 WLR 234, has been affirmed on appeal ([2008] EWCA Civ 574, [2008] RTR 26).   **9.5**

Chapter 10   Limitation

ACCRUAL OF CAUSE OF ACTION

A claim for a summary remedy against a delinquent director for breach of duty to a company   **10.12**
under the Insolvency Act 1986, s. 212, accrues with the breach of duty, not when the liquidator is appointed (*Re Eurocruit Europe Ltd* [2007] EWHC 1433 (Ch), [2008] Bus LR 146). The cause of action accrues to the company, and s. 212 is only procedural in nature.

Accrual in claims for the recovery of land

The principles for establishing adverse possession laid down in *J. A. Pye (Oxford) Ltd v Graham*   **10.13**
[2002] UKHL 30, [2003] 1 AC 419, apply in all claims to recover land (*Ofulue v Bossert* [2008] EWCA Civ 7; [2008] HRLR 20; *Ashe v National Westminster Bank plc* [2008] EWCA Civ 55, [2008] 1 WLR 710). This includes claims by legal mortgagees against mortgagors in possession (*Ashe v National Westminster Bank plc*) and cases where the person claiming adverse possession believed he was a tenant because he had been let into the property by a former tenant (*Ofulue v Bossert*). It also applies in favour of the Crown (Limitation Act 1980, s. 37; *Roberts v Swangrove Estates Ltd* [2008] EWCA Civ 98, [2008] 2 WLR 1111). In *Ashe v National Westminster Bank plc* a mortgagee's legal charge was extinguished under the Limitation Act 1980, s. 17, twelve years after the last payment made by the mortgagor. Permission to appeal to the House of Lords was refused ([2008] 1 WLR 1334).

Money due under statute

A claim to recover sums owed after revocation of a legal aid certificate under the Civil Legal   **10.17**
Aid (General) Regulations 1989 (SI 1989/339), reg. 86, accrues on the date of revocation, not the date when the amount to be recovered has been quantified (*Legal Services Commission v Rasool* [2008] EWCA Civ 154, [2008] 3 All ER 381).

General claims in tort

A claim for damages under the principle in *Francovich v Italy* (cases C-6/90 and C-9/90) [1995] ICR   **10.19**
722) based on an alleged failure of the government to implement Community law accrued when the claimants suffered their personal injuries (*Spencer v Secretary of State for Work and Pensions* [2008] EWCA Civ 750, *The Times*, 24 July 2008). A similar result was achieved in a claim by Lloyd's underwriters in a claim against HM Treasury in *Poole v Her Majesty's Treasury*

[2006] EWHC 2731 (Comm), [2007] 1 All ER (Comm) 255. There is a principle that time does not run until there has been full implementation of a Directive, but this applies only where the conduct of the member State was responsible for the lapse of time which brought the relevant time bar into operation such as to make it inequitable for the State then to rely on the time bar.

Professional negligence

10.20   *Awoyomi v Radford* [2007] EWHC 1671 (QB) is reported at [2008] 3 WLR 34. In *Watkins v Jones Maidment Wilson* [2008] EWCA Civ 134, [2008] PNLR 23, negligent advice resulted in an immediate measurable loss because the claimant lost the chance of negotiating a better agreement, which meant the claim was time-barred. Even if the advice given by the solicitor should have included advice to renegotiate the contract, there was a single event amounting to the breach of duty. In *Shore v Sedgwick Financial Services Ltd* [2008] EWCA Civ 863, *The Times*, 12 August 2008, a claim against financial advisers based on advice to transfer benefits from an occupational pension scheme to a personal pension fund accrued when the benefits were transferred.

Date of knowledge: significant injury

10.25   The burden of proof on the question of whether the claimant knew that an injury was significantly serious within the meaning of the Limitation Act 1980, s. 14(2), rests on the defendant (*Furniss v Firth Brown Tools Ltd* [2008] EWCA Civ 182, LTL 12/3/2008). A person who alleges rape, whether vaginal or anal, objectively has to know at that time that he or she has suffered a significant injury (*Albonetti v Wirral Metropolitan Borough Council* [2008] EWCA Civ 783, LTL 7/7/2008). Time did not run against a claimant who alleged he had suffered industrial deafness while he followed medical advice that his hearing loss was due to wax or an infection (*Field v British Coal Corporation* [2008] EWCA Civ 912, LTL 31/7/2008).

Defective products

10.29   The Limitation Act 1980, s. 11A, requires proceedings to be 'instituted against the producer' of an allegedly defective product within ten years. This does not prevent the court exercising its power to substitute the defendant after the expiry of the ten-year period under s. 35 in cases where the claimant has made a mistake as to the name of the manufacturer of the product (*O'Byrne v Aventis Pasteur MSD Ltd* [2007] EWCA Civ 966, [2008] 1 WLR 1188).

CALCULATING THE LIMITATION PERIOD

Disability

10.33   A potential defendant who is concerned that delay in bringing a claim by a person under disability (as a result of the Limitation Act 1980, s. 28) may prejudice the trial through the evidence becoming stale may force the issue by bringing a claim for a negative declaration as to liability. The person under disability may choose to bring the substantive claim as a counterclaim to those proceedings. The court's decision whether to grant such a negative declaration is a matter of discretion rather than jurisdiction (*Messier Dowty Ltd v Sabena SA* [2000] 1 WLR 2040 as applied in *Eidha v Toropdar* [2008] EWHC 1219 (QB), LTL 6/6/2008).

Concealment

10.35   'Breach of duty' within the meaning of the Limitation Act 1980, s. 32(2), includes a claim under the Insolvency Act 1986, s. 423, that a document was executed as a transaction to defraud a debtor's creditors (*Giles v Rhind* [2008] EWCA Civ 118, [2008] Bus LR 1103).

Acknowledgments and part payments

10.37 A statement of case can amount to an acknowledgment for the purposes of the Limitation Act 1980, s. 29 (*Ofulue v Bossert* [2008] EWCA Civ 7, [2008] HRLR 20). An acknowledgment must, however, be precisely focused on the disputed right (*Surrendra Overseas Ltd v Sri Lanka* [1977] 1 WLR 565).

Defamation: discretionary extension

10.44 The discretion under the Limitation Act 1980, s. 32A, was exercised in favour of granting permission to include claims arising from material published on a website five days beyond the one-year limitation period in *Gentoo Group Ltd v Hanratty* [2008] EWHC 627 (QB), LTL 11/4/2008. The court took into account the connection between the material published outside the limitation period and material published on the same website which came within the primary limitation period, the fact that the relevant evidence was no less cogent through the five-day delay, the seriousness of the alleged libels, and conduct of the defendant in seeking to deflect suspicion that he was responsible for some of the publications.

Personal injury claims: discretionary extension

10.47 **Cross-claim against solicitor**   Possibly negligent discontinuance of the first claim tended towards dismissing an application under the Limitation Act 1980, s. 33 (*Williams v Johnstone* [2008] EWHC 1334 (QB), LTL 26/6/2008).

10.50 **Other factors**   A delay of almost a year after the law was changed by *Horton v Sadler* [2006] UKHL 27, [2007] 1 AC 307, tended against granting more time under the Limitation Act 1980, s. 33 (*Williams v Johnstone* [2008] EWHC 1334 (QB), LTL 26/6/2008).

When *A v Hoare* was reconsidered, following the decision in principle by the House of Lords, the limitation period was disapplied by Coulson J (*A v Hoare* [2008] EWHC 1573 (QB), LTL 15/7/2008).

Chapter 12   Issuing Proceedings

EUROPEAN ORDER FOR PAYMENT

12.11 Regulation (EC) No. 1896/2006 of 12 December 2006 (the 'EOP Regulation') creates a European order for payment ('EOP') procedure with effect from 12 December 2008. The purpose of the Regulation is to simplify, speed up and reduce the costs of litigation in cross-border cases concerning uncontested pecuniary claims by creating the EOP procedure, and to permit the free circulation of EOPs throughout the member States by laying down a common procedure for establishing liability to pay. Compliance with the EOP procedure renders unnecessary any intermediate proceedings in the member State of enforcement prior to recognition and enforcement (recital 9). The procedure established by the EOP Regulation is intended to serve as an additional and optional means for the claimant, who remains free to resort to a procedure provided for by national law. Accordingly, the Regulation neither replaces nor harmonises the existing mechanisms for the recovery of uncontested claims under national law (recital 10).

The EOP Regulation applies to civil and commercial matters in cross-border cases, whatever the nature of the court or tribunal, but with various exceptions set out in art. 1(1) and (2). For this purpose, a cross-border case is one in which at least one of the parties is domiciled or habitually resident in a member State other than the member State of the court seised (art 3(1)).

The EOP Regulation lays down detailed procedural rules, and EOP applications are primarily governed by the EOP Regulation. Where the EOP Regulation is silent, the CPR apply with necessary modifications (PD 78, para. 1.1). When deciding which courts are to have jurisdiction to issue an EOP, member States should take due account of the need to ensure access to justice (recital 12). The procedure is based, to the largest extent possible, on the use of standard forms in any communication between the court and the parties in order to facilitate its administration and enable the use of automatic data processing.

An EOP application form A must be completed in English or accompanied by a translation into English, and filed at court in person or by post (PD 78, para. 2.1). An EOP application made to the High Court will be assigned to the Queen's Bench Division, but that will not prevent the application being transferred where appropriate (para. 2.2). The court seised of an EOP application must examine, as soon as possible and on the basis of the application form, whether the requirements set out in arts 2, 3, 4, 6 and 7 are met and whether the claim appears to be founded (art. 8). The application will be rejected if the requirements are not met (art. 11). If the requirements are met, the court must issue, as soon as possible and normally within 30 days of the lodging of the application, an EOP using standard form E as set out in annex 5 to the EOP Regulation (art. 12(1)). The 30-day period does not include the time taken by the claimant to complete, rectify or modify the application. In the EOP, the defendant is advised of his options to:

(a) pay the amount indicated in the order to the claimant; or
(b) oppose the order by lodging with the court of origin a statement of opposition, to be sent within 30 days of service of the order on him.

Articles 13 to 15 of the EOP Regulation contain rules on service. Where the EOP Regulation is silent on service, the Service Regulation and the CPR apply as appropriate (PD 78, para. 4).

The defendant may lodge a statement of opposition to the EOP with the court of origin using standard form F (as set out in the EOP Regulation, annex 6), which must be supplied to him together with the EOP (art. 16(1)). A statement of opposition has to be sent within 30 days of service of the order on the defendant (art. 16(2)). If a statement of opposition is entered within the time limit laid down in art. 16(2), the proceedings continue before the competent courts of the member State of origin in accordance with the rules of ordinary civil procedure unless the claimant has explicitly requested that the proceedings be terminated in that event (art. 17(1)).

Detailed further provisions can be seen in the EOP Regulation, CPR, Part 78, and PD 78.

Chapter 14   Joinder and Parties

DECEASED PARTIES

Death of party before claim issued

14.12   Before the grant of letters of administration there is a limited power for a person to take essential actions to preserve and protect the deceased's estate. Unless proceedings are necessary for that purpose, a claimant has no right to commence proceedings before the grant, and the court will refuse to give relief to the claimant in such proceedings (*Caudle v LD Law Ltd* [2008] EWHC 374 (QB), [2008] 1 WLR 1540).

CHILDREN AND PROTECTED PARTIES

Protected parties

On the trial of a preliminary issue as to whether a claimant is a protected party, there is no **14.16** requirement that the Official Solicitor be appointed even if neither party asserted that the claimant lacked capacity (*Saulle v Nouvet* [2007] EWHC 2902 (QB), [2008] LS Law Med 201). The Mental Capacity Act 2005 applies to decisions to be made by the Court of Protection, not to decisions in civil litigation under the CPR. However, CPR, Part 21, requires the court to apply the Act's definitions in deciding whether a person is a protected party or a protected beneficiary. The definition within s. 1 is the same as the common law test for capacity as laid down in *Masterman-Lister v Brutton and Co. (Nos. 1 and 2)* [2003] EWCA Civ 70, [2003] 1 WLR 1511, and the burden of proof rests on the party asserting a lack of capacity.

BANKRUPTCY

Even though under the Insolvency Act 1986 assets remain vested in the bankrupt until the **14.25** appointment of the trustee in bankruptcy, the bankrupt has no standing to make applications in litigation in the interim period (*Dadourian Group International Inc. v Simms* [2008] EWHC 723 (Ch), LTL 6/5/2008).

A possible solution where a trustee in bankruptcy refuses to act is for the bankrupt to challenge the trustee's decision under the Insolvency Act 1986, s. 303 (*Dadourian Group International Inc. v Simms*).

COMPANIES

Derivative claims

Derivative claims may also be made by a beneficiary of a trust on behalf of the trustees and **14.27** a beneficiary under a will on behalf of the estate, but such claims are not covered by CPR, rr. 19.9 to 19.9F. See *Roberts v Gill and Co.* [2008] EWCA Civ 803, *The Times*, 18 August 2008.

INTERPLEADER PROCEEDINGS

Introduction

Participation by a property holder as an applicant in interpleader proceedings does not **14.73** ordinarily amount to a submission to the jurisdiction, because the purpose of interpleader proceedings is to gain the protection of the court from the competing claimants (*Australia v Peacekeeper International FZC UAE* [2008] EWHC 1220 (QB), LTL 9/6/2008).

ADDITION AND SUBSTITUTION OF PARTIES

Addition of parties

A party may be added to a claim under CPR, r. 19.2(2), even if none of the existing parties to **14.80** the litigation could assert a substantive claim against the new party (*Dunlop Haywards (DHL) Ltd v Erinaceous Insurance Services Ltd* [2008] EWHC 520 (Comm), [2008] NPC 80). Where such a claim can be asserted, CPR, Part 20, is always available.

Addition or substitution of a party after the expiry of the limitation period

14.87   *Martin v Kaisary* [2005] EWCA Civ 594 is reported at [2006] PIQR P58.

Adding a new party after limitation will not be 'necessary' within the meaning of the Limitation Act 1980, s. 35(5)(b), and CPR, r. 19.5(2)(b), if the applicant has, on the existing statement of case, a claim vested in himself, even if a wider claim might be possible with the amendment (*Roberts v Gill and Co.* [2008] EWCA Civ 803, *The Times*, 18 August 2008).

14.88   **Correcting a mistake**   Where the mistake is as to the defendant's name as opposed to its identity, substitution will be 'necessary' for the purposes of the Limitation Act 1980, s. 35(5) and (6) (*O'Byrne v Aventis Pasteur MSD Ltd* [2007] EWCA Civ 966, [2008] 1 WLR 1188). The fact the claimant became aware that the named defendant was not the manufacturer in a defective product claim is not relevant on the question of whether it is necessary to substitute the actual manufacturer (*O'Byrne v Aventis Pasteur MSD Ltd*). An appeal to the House of Lords has been stayed pending a further reference to the European Court of Justice (*O'Byrne v Aventis Pasteur MSD Ltd* [2008] UKHL 34, LTL 12/6/2008).

14.91   **Alteration of capacity**   If an amendment after limitation requires the addition of a new party as well as a change of capacity, the principles discussed at **14.87** have to be complied with as well as those on change of capacity (*Roberts v Gill and Co.* [2008] EWCA Civ 803, *The Times*, 18 August 2008).

Chapter 15   Filing and Service

INTRODUCTION

15.1   As the text says at 15.1, the rules on service in the CPR have probably been among the least successful of the Woolf reforms. They have generated a large volume of case law, partly as a result of internal inconsistencies in the rules, and partly through concepts from the pre-CPR rules being carried forward into the CPR scheme on an imperfect basis. To cure the problems, the whole of CPR, Part 6, has been replaced with effect from 1 October 2008 (by the Civil Procedure (Amendment) Rules 2008, SI 2008/2178).

There are numerous consequential minor changes to other rules which make cross-references to Part 6. These are CPR, rr. 2.3(1), 7.4(3), 7.5, 7.6, 10.3(2), 10.5, 12.3(3), 12.4(4), 12.10, 12.11, 13.3, 14.2, 15.4(2), 16.5, 20.13, 21.1, 21.5, 21.8, 26.3, 40.4, 42.2, 45.5, 54.28B, 55.8, 55.23, 56.3, 57.4, 57.16, 58.6, 58.10, 59.5, 59.9, 61.4, 61.11, 62.5, 62.16, 62.18, 62.20, 63.16, 65.18, 74.6; RSC ord. 115, rr. 17 and 33, CCR ord. 27, rr. 5 and 17, CCR ord. 28, rr. 2 and 3, CCR ord. 29, r. 1 and CCR ord. 33, r. 4.

Table 15.1 in this supplement compares the pre-October 2008 ('old rule') and October 2008 onwards ('new rule') CPR provisions on service. **Table 15.2** in this supplement makes the same comparison for practice directions.

Table 15.1 Comparison of CPR provisions on service before and from 1 October 2008

Subject	Before 1 October 2008	On and after 1 October 2008	Comments
Part 6 rules about service apply generally	r. 6.1	r. 6.1	Minor wording change.
Interpretation		r. 6.2	New. Partially taken from old r. 6.7(3).
II Service of the claim form in the jurisdiction			Section heading introduced in new rule.

Subject	Before 1 October 2008	On and after 1 October 2008	Comments
Methods of service	r. 6.2	rr. 6.3, 6.20	Old rule covered service of all documents. New r. 6.3 is limited to service of the claim form (which includes a petition (r. 6.2(c)). New r. 6.20 deals with service of other documents. While service by document exchange falls into the same sub-para. as first class post in new rr. 6.3(1)(b) and 6.20(1)(b), it is kept separate in the provisions dealing with when DX service may be used (PD 6A, para. 2.1) and deemed service in r. 6.23. Alternative service (new rr. 6.15, 6.27) is expressly brought into new rr. 6.3, 6.20.
Who is to serve the claim form	r. 6.3	rr. 6.4, 6.21	Old rule covered service of all documents. New r. 6.4 is limited to service of the claim form. New r. 6.21 deals with service of other documents. Minor wording changes. Old r. 6.3(1)(e) on court failure to serve applies in the new rule only to claim forms (new r. 6.4(4)), and now expressly says the court will not attempt to serve again.
Personal service	r. 6.4	rr. 6.5, 6.22	New rules reorganise old rule. Old r. 6.4(2) on solicitor authorised to accept service is new r. 6.7(1)(b).
Where to serve the claim form — general provisions	rr. 6.5(1); 6.13(1)	r. 6.6	Expanded. New r. 6.6(2) (address at which the defendant may be served) is equivalent of old r. 6.13(1).
Address for service	r. 6.5(2)–(5), (7)	r. 6.23	New rules reorganise old rule provisions. An email address or electronic identification given by a party will be deemed to be at the address for service (new r. 6.23(6)).
Service of the claim form on a solicitor	rr. 6.4(2); 6.5(3)–(5); 6.13(2)	r. 6.7	New rule reorganises provisions of old rules.
Service of the claim form where the defendant gives an address at which the defendant may be served	r. 6.5(4)	r. 6.8	Reworded.
Service of the claim form where the defendant does not give an address at which the defendant may be served	r. 6.5(6)	r. 6.9	Substantially expanded. Where a claimant has reason to believe that the address of the defendant referred to in the table in new r. 6.9(2) is an address at which the defendant no longer resides or carries on business, the claimant must take reasonable steps to ascertain the address of the defendant's current residence or place of business (see new r. 6.9(3) to (6)).
Service in proceedings against the Crown	r. 6.5 (8)	rr. 6.10; 6.23(7)	Reworded.
Service of the claim form by contractually agreed method	r. 6.15	r. 6.11	Minor changes, including service at a place specified in the contract.

(continued)

Subject	Before 1 October 2008	On and after 1 October 2008	Comments
Service of the claim form relating to a contract on an agent of a principal who is out of the jurisdiction	r. 6.16	r. 6.12	Reorganised, with specified requirements for the evidence in support (new r. 6.12(2)(a)).
Service on children and protected parties	r. 6.6	rr. 6.13, 6.25	New r. 6.13 deals with service of the claim form, r. 6.25 with other documents. Substantially reorganised and reworded.
Deemed service	r. 6.7	rr. 6.14; 7.5; 6.26; PD 6A, paras 10.1–10.7	Under new r. 6.14, a claim form which is served in accordance with Part 6 is deemed to be served on the second business day after completion of the relevant step under new r. 7.5(1). For other documents, new r. 6.26 has a similar table of deemed dates as old r. 6.7. A number of worked examples are given in new PD 6A, paras 10.1–10.7
Service by an alternative method or at an alternative place	r. 6.8	rr. 6.15; 6.27	New rr. 6.15 (claim forms) and 6.27 (other documents) are expanded to provide for service at an alternative place as well as by an alternative method.
Power of court to dispense with service	r. 6.9	r. 6.16; 6.28	New rules (r. 6.16 claim forms; r. 6.28 other documents) expand on old r. 6.9, and add the test that there must be exceptional circumstances.
Notice of court service and certificate of service	rr. 6.10, 6.14	rr. 6.17; 6.29; PD 6A, para. 7.1	New r. 6.17 deals with certificates of service etc. relating to claim forms, r. 6.29 with other documents. Both are revised on amalgamating old rr. 6.10 and 6.14. Where the court serves a claim form, it will send to the claimant a notice including the date on which the claim form is deemed served (new r. 6.17(1)). A claimant's certificate of service of the claim form must be filed within 21 days of service of the particulars of claim unless all the defendants have filed acknowledgments by that time (new r. 6.17(2)).
Notification of outcome of postal service by the court	r. 6.11	r. 6.18	Slightly expanded to clarify.
Notice of non-service by bailiff	r. 6.11A	r. 6.19	Slightly revised.
III Service of documents other than the claim form in the United Kingdom			Section heading introduced in new rule.
Change of address for service	PD 6, para. 7	r. 6.24	Where the address for service of a party changes, that party must give notice in writing of the change as soon as it has taken place to the court and every other party (new r. 6.24).

Subject	Before 1 October 2008	On and after 1 October 2008	Comments
IV Service of the claim form and other documents out of the jurisdiction			Equivalent to old Section III.
Scope of this Section	r. 6.17	r. 6.30	
Interpretation	r. 6.18	r. 6.31	Reorganised.
Service of the claim form where the permission of the court is not required — Scotland and Northern Ireland	r. 6.25 (4); PD 6B, para. 3.1, 3.2	r. 6.32	Revised.
Service of the claim form where the permission of the court is not required — out of the United Kingdom	r. 6.19(1)–(2)	r. 6.33	Revised.
Notice of statement of grounds where the permission of the court is not required for service	r. 6.19(3)	r. 6.34	Expanded.
Period for responding to the claim form where permission was not required for service	rr. 6.22, 6. 23	r. 6.35	Amalgamated.
Service of the claim form where the permission of the court is required	r. 6.20	r. 6.36	The detailed grounds for seeking permission to serve outside the jurisdiction in old r. 6.20 are now in new PD 6B, para 3.1.
Application for permission to serve the claim form out of the jurisdiction	r. 6.21	r. 6.37	Slightly expanded.
Service of documents other than the claim form — permission		r. 6.38	New. Subject to other provisions within new r. 6.38, where the permission of the court is required for the claimant to serve the claim form out of the jurisdiction, the claimant must obtain permission to serve any other document in the proceedings out of the jurisdiction. The requirement in new r. 6.23 to give an address for service within the jurisdiction limits the need to resort to r. 6.38.
Service of application notice on a non-party to the proceedings		r. 6.39	New.
Methods of service — general provisions	r. 6.24	r. 6.40	Expanded.
Service in accordance with the Service Regulation	r. 6.26A	r. 6.41	Expanded.

(continued)

Subject	Before 1 October 2008	On and after 1 October 2008	Comments
Service through foreign governments, judicial authorities and British Consular authorities	r. 6.25	r. 6.42	Revised.
Procedure where service is to be through foreign governments, judicial authorities and British Consular authorities	r. 6.26	r. 6.43	Revised.
Service of claim form or other document on a State	r. 6.27	r. 6.44	Reorganised.
Translation of claim form or other document	r. 6.28	r. 6.45	Revised.
Undertaking to be responsible for expenses	r. 6.29	r. 6.46	Unchanged.
Proof of service before obtaining judgment	r. 6.31	r. 6.47	Slightly revised.
V Service of documents from foreign courts or tribunals			Equivalent to old Section IV.
Scope of this Section	r. 6.32(1)	r. 6.48	Unchanged.
Interpretation	r. 6.32(2)	r. 6.49	Slightly revised.
Request for service	r. 6.33	r. 6.50	Slightly revised.
Method of service	r. 6.34	r. 6.51	Slightly revised.
After service	r. 6.35	r. 6.52	Slightly revised.
Service of a claim form	r. 7.5	r. 7.5	Substantially amended. For a claim form served within the jurisdiction, the claimant must complete the step required by the table in r. 7.5(1) in relation to the particular method of service chosen, before 12.00 midnight on the calendar day four months after the date of issue of the claim form (new r. 7.5(1)). The period is 6 months where service is outside the jurisdiction (r. 7.5(2)).
Extension of time for serving a claim form	r. 7.6	r. 7.6	New r. 7.6 provides for extending time for compliance with r. 7.5 (act constituting the method service), rather than the time for serving (old r. 7.5).

Table 15.2 Practice directions on service before and from 1 October 2008

	Before 1 October 2008	On and after 1 October 2008	Comments
When service may be by document exchange	PD 6, para. 2.1	PD 6A, para. 2.1	
How service is effected by post, an alternative service provider or DX	PD 6, para. 2.2	PD 6A, para. 3.1	

	Before 1 October 2008	On and after 1 October 2008	Comments
Service by fax or other electronic means	PD 6, paras 3.1–3.4	PD 6A, paras 4.1–4.3	
Service on members of the regular forces and United States Air Force	PD 6, para. 5	PD 6A, para. 5.1	
Personal service on a company or other corporation	PD 6, paras 6.1, 6.2	PD 6A, paras 6.1, 6.2	
Service by the court	PD 6, paras 8.1–8.3	PD 6A, paras 8.1, 8.2	
Application for an order for service by an alternative method or at an alternative place	PD 6, para. 9.1	PD 6A, paras 9.1–9.3	
Service on members of the regular forces	PD 6, annex	PD 6A, annex	
Service out of the jurisdiction where permission of the court is not required	PD 6B, paras 1.1–1.5	PD 6B, para. 2.1	New PD 6B, para. 2.1, provides that where new CPR, r. 6.34, applies, the claimant must file form N510 when filing the claim form. This replaces the detailed jurisdictional endorsements in old PD 6B, paras 1.1–1.3C.
Service out of the jurisdiction where permission is required		PD 6B, para. 3.1	Equivalent to the old r. 6.20.
Documents to be filed under r. 6.43(2)(c)	PD 6B, paras 2.1, 2.2	PD 6B, paras 4.1, 4.2	
Service in a Commonwealth State or British overseas territory	PD 6B, paras 3.1, 3.2	PD 6B, paras 5.1, 5.2	
Period for responding to a claim form	PD 6B, paras 7.1–7.4	PD 6B, paras 6.1, 6.6	
Period for responding to an application notice	PD 6B, para. 8.1	PD 6B, para. 7.1	
Further information	PD 6B, paras 10.1, 10.2	PD 6B, para. 8.2	
Table of response periods for different countries	PD 6B, table	PD 6B, table	

Service under the new rules

With effect from 1 October 2008, the service rules in CPR, Part 6, will provide for four schemes dealing with service of documents. There are allied schemes dealing with service under the Companies and Insolvency Acts and EU Regulations. The system is as follows:

(a) Service of a claim form (or other originating process) within the jurisdiction (CPR, rr. 6.3 to 6.19). Secondary schemes apply to service on a company at its registered office (Companies Acts 1985 and 2006) and of insolvency proceedings (Insolvency Act 1986 and Insolvency Rules).

(b) Service of documents other than a claim form within the jurisdiction (CPR, rr. 6.20 to 6.29). There are again secondary schemes under the Companies Acts and Insolvency legislation.

(c) Service of a claim form and other documents outside the jurisdiction (CPR, rr. 6.30 to 6.47). These rules are supplemented by Regulation (EC) No. 1393/2007 ('the Service Regulation'), and also by rules on service contained in Regulation (EC) No 1896/2006 of 12 December 2006 (the 'EOP Regulation') (see **12.11** in this supplement) and Regulation (EC) No 861/2007 of 11 July 2007 (the 'ESCP Regulation') (see **43.1** in this supplement).

(d) Service of documents from foreign courts and tribunals (CPR, rr. 6.48 to 6.52).

For service outside the jurisdiction, see **chapter 16** in this supplement.

The provisions in CPR, Part 6, and PD 6A, dealing with service of claim forms are similar to the rules dealing with service of other documents, but there are detailed minor differences, principally on the question of deemed service.

Methods of service

Both CPR, r. 6.3 (claim forms), and r. 6.20 (other documents), provide for the following methods of service which comply with the CPR:

(a) personal service;
(b) first class post, document exchange or other service which provides for delivery on the next business day;
(c) leaving the document at a place specified in the rules prescribing where documents must be served — in effect this involves hand delivering the document at the defendant's address;
(d) fax or other means of electronic communication; and
(e) alternative methods of service authorised by the court.

Service on companies and limited liability partnerships may be effected under CPR, Part 6, or under the Companies Acts. Service under the Companies Acts operates outside the CPR, and is effected at the company's registered office.

There is a hierarchy of methods of service. For claim forms it is:

(1) personal service has to be used where an enactment, rule or practice direction specifically so requires (CPR, r. 6.5(1));
(2) if not, service has to be effected on the other side's solicitor (r. 6.7, provided the defendant has given in writing the business address within the jurisdiction of a solicitor as an address at which the defendant may be served with the claim form, or a solicitor acting for the defendant has notified the claimant in writing that the solicitor is instructed by the defendant to accept service of the claim form on behalf of the defendant at a business address within the jurisdiction);
(3) if not, service is effected on the address given by the other side for service (r. 6.8);
(4) otherwise, any of methods (a) to (d) above can be used;
(5) as a last resort, an order for service by an alternative method or at an alternative place should be sought under r. 6.15.

For other documents, the hierarchy is:

(1) personal service has to be used where an enactment, rule or practice direction specifically so requires (r. 6.22(1));
(2) if not, service has to be effected on the other side's solicitor if a United Kingdom based solicitor is acting for the party (r. 6.23(2)(a));
(3) if not, service is effected at the other side's residence or place of business (r. 6.23(2)(b));
(4) in the absence of any of the above, each party has to give an address for service within the United Kingdom (r. 6.23(3));

(5) otherwise, any of the methods in (a) to (d) above can be used;

(6) as a last resort, an order for service by an alternative method or at an alternative place should be sought under r. 6.27.

Personal service on an individual is effected by leaving it with that individual (r. 6.5(a)). Personal service on a company is effected by leaving it with a person holding a senior position within the company or corporation (r. 6.5(3)(b)). Personal service on a partnership is effected by leaving it with a partner, or a person who, at the time of service, has the control or management of the partnership business, at its principal place of business (r. 6.5(3)(c)).

Service by document exchange (DX) is only allowed (PD 6A, para 2.1) if:

(a) the address at which the party is to be served includes a numbered box at a DX, or

(b) the writing paper of the party who is to be served or of the solicitor acting for that party sets out a DX box number, and (in either case)

(c) the party or the solicitor acting for that party has not indicated in writing that they are unwilling to accept service by DX.

Service by fax or other electronic means is only permitted in accordance with PD 6A, para. 4.1. This provides that the party who is to be served or the solicitor acting for that party must previously have indicated in writing to the party serving:

(a) that the party to be served or the solicitor is willing to accept service by fax or other electronic means. The following are sufficient written indications for the purpose:

   (i) a fax number set out on the writing paper of the solicitor acting for the party to be served;

   (ii) an email address set out on the writing paper of the solicitor acting for the party to be served but only where it is stated that the email address may be used for service; or

   (iii) a fax number, email address or electronic identification set out on a statement of case or a response to a claim filed with the court; and

(b) the fax number, email address or other electronic identification to which it must be sent. The fax number must be at the party's address for service (CPR, r. 6.23(5)), and an email address is deemed to be at the address for service (r. 6.23(6)).

Where a document is served by electronic means, the party serving the document need not in addition send or deliver a hard copy (PD 6A, para. 4.3).

Service of a claim form where the defendant does not give an address

The fall-back position where personal service, service on a solicitor, and service at an address given by the defendant are not available is set out in CPR, r. 6.9 (see **table 15.3** in this supplement). This sets out addresses where a claim form can be served at a place as opposed to on a person.

Table 15.3 Service of a claim form if the defendant does not give an address

Nature of defendant to be served	Place of service
1. Individual	Usual or last known residence.
2. Individual being sued in the name of a business	Usual or last known residence of the individual; or principal or last known place of business.
3. Individual being sued in the business name of a partnership	Usual or last known residence of the individual; or principal or last known place of business of the partnership.
4. Limited liability partnership	Principal office of the partnership; or *(continued)*

Nature of defendant to be served	Place of service
	any place of business of the partnership within the jurisdiction which has a real connection with the claim.
5. Corporation (other than a company) incorporated in England and Wales	Principal office of the corporation; or any place within the jurisdiction where the corporation carries on its activities and which has a real connection with the claim.
6. Company registered in England and Wales	Principal office of the company; or any place of business of the company within the jurisdiction which has a real connection with the claim.
7. Any other company or corporation	Any place within the jurisdiction where the corporation carries on its activities; or any place of business of the company within the jurisdiction.

Service at a last known address

The entries in the table at CPR, r. 6.9(2), allowing service at a former address which is the one last known to the claimant, are regarded as a last resort. Ultimately service at a last known address is effective even though the defendant never receives the documents (*Collier v Williams* [2006] EWCA Civ 20, [2006] 1 WLR 1945). To mitigate the potential unfairness, r. 6.9(3) provides that in this situation the claimant must take reasonable steps to ascertain the address of the defendant's current residence or place of business ('current address') (confirming *Mersey Docks Property Holdings Ltd v Kilgour* [2004] EWHC 1638 (TCC), [2004] BLR 412). Where, having taken the reasonable steps required by r. 6.9(3), the claimant ascertains the defendant's current address, the claim form must be served at that address (r. 6.9(4)(a)). Service at the defendant's usual or last known address is only allowed if, after making enquiries:

(a) the claimant cannot ascertain the defendant's current residence or place of business; and
(b) cannot ascertain an alternative place or an alternative method for the purposes of an application under r. 6.15 (r. 6.9(6)).

Period of validity of a claim form

Where a claim form is served within the jurisdiction, CPR, r. 7.5(1), requires the claimant to complete the step required by **table 15.4**, before 12.00 midnight on the calendar day four months after the date of issue of the claim form. (This form of words means that the day of issue of the claim form is not counted in calculating the four months).

Table 15.4 Steps which must be taken within four months of issue of a claim form

Method of service	Step required
First class post, document exchange or other service which provides for delivery on the next business day.	Posting, leaving with, delivering to or collection by the relevant service provider.
Delivery of the document to or leaving it at the relevant place.	Delivering to or leaving the document at the relevant place.
Personal service under r. 6.5.	Completing the relevant step required by r. 6.5(3).
Fax.	Completing the transmission of the fax.
Other electronic method.	Sending the email or other electronic transmission.

Deemed service of a claim form

A claim form served in accordance with CPR, Part 6, is deemed to be served on the second business day after completion of the relevant step under r. 7.5(1) (r. 6.14). The phrase 'is deemed to be served' creates an irrebuttable presumption of service on the date calculated in accordance with r. 6.14 (*Cranfield v Bridgegrove Ltd* [2003] EWCA Civ 656, [2003] 1 WLR 2441). The effect of rr. 7.5(1) and 6.14 is that, in serving within the period of validity, the claimant does not have to be concerned with how long it takes for the claim form to reach the defendant, or even if it ever does reach the defendant. Also, full use of the periods available means that a claim form may be validly served where deemed service takes effect four months and two business days after issue.

Deemed service of other documents

A document, other than a claim form, served in accordance with CPR, Part 6, is deemed to be served on the day shown in the table set out in r. 6.26 (**table 15.5**).

Table 15.5 Deemed dates of service

Method of service	Deemed date of service
1. First class post (or other service which provides for delivery on the next business day).	The second day after it was posted, left with, delivered to or collected by the relevant service provider provided that day is a business day; or if not, the next business day after that day.
2. Document exchange.	The second day after it was left with, delivered to or collected by the relevant service provider provided that day is a business day; or if not, the next business day after that day.
3. Delivering the document to or leaving it at a permitted address.	If it is delivered to or left at the permitted address on a business day before 4.30 p.m., on that day; or in any other case, on the next business day after that day.
4. Fax.	If the transmission of the fax is completed on a business day before 4.30 p.m., on that day; or in any other case, on the next business day after the day on which it was transmitted.
5. Other electronic method.	If the email or other electronic transmission is sent on a business day before 4.30 p.m., on that day; or in any other case, on the next business day after the day on which it was sent.
6. Personal service.	If the document is served personally before 4.30 p.m. on a business day, on that day; or in any other case, on the next business day after that day.

This table uses the expressions 'day' (which means a calendar day) and 'business day', which is defined in r. 6.2(b) as any day except Saturday, Sunday, a bank holiday, Good Friday or Christmas Day. 'Bank holiday' means a bank holiday under the Banking and Financial Dealings Act 1971 in the part of the United Kingdom where service is to take place (r. 6.2(a)). Rule 2.8 (which excludes weekends and public holidays when calculating periods of five days or less) does not apply here (*Anderton v Clwyd County Council (No. 2)* [2002] EWCA Civ 933, [2002] 1 WLR 3174), because nothing is 'done'.

There is a latent ambiguity in **table 15.5** over whether the phrase 'provided that day is a business day' applies to the date (for example) that the document is posted, or the deemed date of service, or both. There is a slight indication it is both in example 1 in PD 6A, para. 10.2, which says: 'Where the document is posted (by first class post) on a Monday (a business day), the day of deemed service is the following Wednesday (a business day)'. It is, however, clear from example 6 in PD 6A that the phrase only refers to the deemed date of service, not to the date of posting (etc.). Example 6 says: 'Where the document is posted (by first class post) on a bank holiday Monday, the day of deemed service is the following Wednesday (a business day).'

Failure to update rule 47.12(3) and (4)

Remarkably, CPR, r. 47.12(3) and (4) (which deal with setting aside a default costs certificate), have not been changed by the Civil Procedure (Amendment) Rules 2008 (SI 2008/2178). These provisions are based on the view that service is not effected if a document is returned undelivered through the post, which is contrary to the Court of Appeal authorities on deemed service (see **15.36** and **15.37**), which say the methods of service in Part 6 create an irrebuttable presumption of due service. This is especially remarkable because r. 47.12 was amended by SI 2008/2178 to add a new para. (5) (on pro bono costs). The result is that r. 47.12(3) and (4) remain in a form which is inconsistent with the rest of the CPR on service.

Inconsistency of the deemed service rule with EU Regulations

It is also interesting that at the same time as these changes were made, CPR, Part 78, was introduced to give effect to Regulation (EC) No. 1896/2006 of 12 December 2006 creating a European order for payment procedure. Recital (19) provides:

'Due to differences between member States' rules of civil procedure and especially those governing the service of documents, it is necessary to lay down a specific and detailed definition of minimum standards that should apply in the context of the European order for payment procedure. In particular, as regards the fulfilment of those standards, any method based on legal fiction should not be considered sufficient for the service of the European order for payment.'

Of course the basis of much of the new CPR, Part 6, and in particular the deemed service rules at rr. 6.14 and 6.26, are founded on a fiction of service. There may be further expansion of harmonisation measures from the EU, the Community having set itself the objective of maintaining and developing an area of freedom, security and justice in which the free movement of persons is ensured. For the gradual establishment of such an area, the Community is to adopt, *inter alia*, measures in the field of judicial cooperation in civil matters having cross-border implications and needed for the proper functioning of the internal market. According to art. 65(c) of the Treaty establishing the European Community, these measures are to include measures eliminating obstacles to the good functioning of civil proceedings, if necessary by promoting the compatibility of the rules on civil procedure applicable in the member states.

TIME FOR SERVING A CLAIM FORM

Period of validity

15.2 The period of validity of a claim form remains at four months after the date of issue of the claim form for a domestic claim form (new CPR, r. 7.5(1), introduced from 1 October 2008 by the Civil Procedure (Amendment) Rules 2008, SI 2008/2178). It is six months for a claim form which is to be served outside the jurisdiction (new r. 7.5(2)).

Calculating the period of validity

For claim forms served within the jurisdiction, the day of issue of the claim form is not **15.3** counted in calculating the four-month period of validity in CPR, r. 7.5(1) (as substituted with effect from 1 October 2008 by the Civil Procedure (Amendment) Rules 2008, SI 2008/2178). This follows from the use of the phrase 'after the date of issue of the claim form' (*Smith v Probyn* (2000) *The Times*, 29 March 2000). All the claimant has to do under the new rule is to take the step which will effect service within this four-month period ('the claimant must complete the step required by [**table 15.4**]'). Provided the claimant knows the defendant's address within r. 6.6, r. 7.5(1) now gives the claimant full control on compliance with the four-month period free from shortcomings in the delivery provider or evasion by the defendant. Deemed service under new r. 6.14 (on the second business day after the relevant step) can take effect after the four-month period without affecting the validity of service.

For claim forms for service outside the jurisdiction, r. 7.5(2) provides with effect from 1 October 2008: 'Where the claim form is to be served out of the jurisdiction, the claim form must be served in accordance with Section IV of Part 6 within 6 months of the date of issue'. This has two significant drafting differences from r. 7.5(1):

(a) Service under r. 7.5(2) must be effected within six months 'of the date of issue' rather than 'after the date of issue' of the claim form. Use of this phrase may mean that the day of issue has to be counted.
(b) Under r. 7.5(2), service must be completed (under the rules for service outside the jurisdiction) by the end of the six-month period of validity (subject to any renewal under r. 7.6).

EXTENDING TIME FOR SERVING A CLAIM FORM

Grounds on which the court will grant an extension

There is a new CPR, r. 7.6, with effect from 1 October 2008 (by the Civil Procedure **15.9** (Amendment) Rules 2008, SI 2008/2178). It is reworded for consistency with the new r. 7.5, but is unchanged in substance. However, the full control given to the claimant in complying with r. 7.5(1) (see **15.3** in this supplement) will mean that it will be extremely difficult to fulfil the requirement in r. 7.6(3)(b) of taking all reasonable steps to comply with r. 7.5(1). Extensions other than in cases where the defendant is evading service or where the court fails to serve will be difficult to justify.

Dispensing with service because of problems with serving

The decision to dispense with service under CPR, r. 6.9, in *Olafsson v Gissurarson (No. 2)* [2006] **15.12** EWHC 3214 (QB) has been upheld on appeal ([2008] EWCA Civ 152, [2008] 1 All ER (Comm) 1106), because it was a truly exceptional case with the merest technical defect in the rules on service.

Although the court has a discretionary power under CPR, r. 6.9, to dispense with service of documents required in the procedures under the Extradition Act 2003, there are powerful reasons why the discretion should not be exercised where the effect would be to override any of the time limits laid down by that Act (*Mucelli v Albania* [2007] EWHC 2632 (Admin), [2008] 2 All ER 340). Exceptionally, r. 6.9 (and also r. 3.10) were applied to dispense with service and correct a defect in procedure in an Extradition Act 2003 case where the document was transmitted by fax, with the transmission starting before the 4 p.m. deadline, but not ending until shortly after 4 p.m. in *Moulai v Deputy Public Prosecutor in Créteil, France* [2008] EWHC 1024 (Admin), [2008] 3 All ER 226.

FILING DOCUMENTS

Inspecting the court file

15.16 **Public right to access to court register and to court documents** The right of access to statements of case under CPR, r. 5.4C, extends to the acknowledgment of service and detailed grounds for contesting a claim for judicial review (*R (Corner House Research) v Director of the Serious Fraud Office* [2008] EWHC 246 (Admin), [2008] 3 WLR 568).

SERVICE BY A PARTY

15.21 With effect from 1 October 2008, the need to file a certificate of service with the particulars of claim within seven days of a claimant himself serving the particulars of claim (CPR, r. 7.4(3)) has been removed by the Civil Procedure (Amendment) Rules 2008 (SI 2008/2178). A claimant's certificate of service of the claim form must instead be filed within 21 days of service of the particulars of claim unless all the defendants have filed acknowledgments by that time (new r. 6.17(2)).

Chapter 16   Service Outside the Jurisdiction

INTRODUCTION

16.1 The procedural rules in CPR, Part 6, on service outside the jurisdiction have been replaced with effect from 1 October 2008. Care should be taken of the notes issued by the Ministry of Justice with the 47th Update, which misleadingly say that Part 6 'is revised with the exception of service out of the jurisdiction'. In fact, all the provisions dealing with service out of the jurisdiction have a number of technical changes. The most fundamental difference is that the grounds on which service outside the jurisdiction may be granted with permission have been moved from the old CPR, r. 6.20, to the new PD 6B, para. 3.1.

Tables 15.1 and 15.2 of this supplement includes cross-references between the old and new rules on service out of the jurisdiction.

CASES OUTSIDE THE GENERAL RULES

Under the Jurisdiction and Judgments Regulation

16.14 **Enforcement of judgments** Regulation (EC) No. 44/2001 (the Jurisdiction and Judgments Regulation), art. 22(5), is concerned with actual enforcement, so does not apply to freezing injunctions and receivers by way of equitable enforcement (*Masri v Consolidated Contractors International UK Ltd (No. 2)* [2008] EWCA Civ 303, [2008] 2 Lloyd's Rep 128). An order under CPR, r. 71.2, for the examination of a foreign officer of a judgment debtor comes within art. 30(2), and can be served outside the jurisdiction without permission (*Masri v Consolidated Contractors International Co. SAL* [2008] EWCA Civ 876, LTL 28/7/2008).

JURISDICTION UNDER THE JURISDICTION AND JUDGMENTS REGULATION

Scope of the Jurisdiction and Judgments Regulation

16.16 A claim which is brought by or against a public law body acting in the exercise of its public powers is not a 'civil [or] commercial matter' within the meaning of the Regulation (EC) No. 44/2001 (the Jurisdiction and Judgments Regulation), art. 1(1) (*Grovit v De Nederlandsche Bank NV* [2007] EWCA Civ 953, [2008] 1 WLR 51). In this case a decision by the central bank to refuse registration of a money transaction business was held to be a public law decision.

Matrimonial cases are governed by Council Regulation (EC) No. 2201/2003 on jurisdiction and enforcement in matrimonial and parental responsibility matters rather than Regulation (EC) No. 44/2001, and see *Proceedings brought by C* (case C-435/06) [2008] 3 WLR 419.

An application for an ancillary order against a non-party for disclosure of assets pursuant to a freezing injunction (see **38.25**) does not amount to 'suing' the non-party for the purposes of the Jurisdiction and Judgments Regulation (*Masri v Consolidated Contractors International Co. SAL* [2008] EWCA Civ 876, LTL 28/7/2008). Jurisdiction for such an application is based on jurisdiction in the application for the freezing injunction.

Domicile: the general rule

16.17 Domicile under the Jurisdiction and Judgments Regulation is independent of the concept at common law. Under the Jurisdiction and Judgments Regulation the concept aims at identifying a location where the potential defendant has a real connection at the relevant time (*Ministry of Defence and Support for the Armed Forces for the Islamic Republic of Iran v FAZ Aviation Ltd* [2007] EWHC 1042 (Comm), [2008] 1 All ER (Comm) 372). Identification of the company's 'seat' will usually be straightforward, but domicile can also be established from its principal place of business. This is usually where corporate authority (shareholders and directors) is located, i.e., where it is controlled and managed.

Contract

16.19 **Main provision**   A claim brought under the Contracts (Rights of Third Parties) Act 1999 is a matter relating to a contract within the Jurisdiction and Judgments Regulation, art. 5(1) (*WPP Holdings Italy SRL v Benatti* [2007] EWCA Civ 263, [2007] 1 WLR 2316).

16.21 **Place of performance of obligation**   Unless otherwise agreed, in the case of the sale of goods the place of performance is the place where the goods were or should have been delivered. In the case of the provision of services, it is the place where the services were or should have been provided (Jurisdiction and Judgments Regulation, art. 5(1)(b)).

In a claim relating to the sale of goods where the contract provided for delivery to a number of locations, the 'place of delivery' under art. 5(1) is the place with the closest link with the contract. In general this is the principal place of delivery determined on the basis of economic criteria, which is a matter to be decided by the domestic court seised of the proceedings (*Color Drack GmbH v Lexx International Vertriebs GmbH* (case C-386/05) [2008] 1 All ER (Comm) 168). If there is no principal place of delivery, each of the delivery points can found the basis for jurisdiction under art. 5(1), giving the claimant a choice of where to litigate (*Color Drack GmbH v Lexx International Vertriebs GmbH*). In an FOB contract, risk and property pass to the buyer on shipment, and delivery as a result is effected on shipment by virtue of the Sale of Goods Act 1979, s. 32(1) (*Scottish and Newcastle International Ltd v Othon Ghalanos Ltd* [2008] UKHL 11, [2008] Bus LR 583).

The place of performance of a warranty as to an existing state of affairs is the place where that state of affairs was required to exist (*Crucial Music Corporation v Klondyke Management AG* [2007] EWHC 1782 (Ch), [2008] Bus LR 327).

16.25 **Jurisdiction agreements**   Jurisdiction was conferred by the Jurisdiction and Judgments Regulation, art. 23, in accordance with a jurisdiction clause contained in standard terms and conditions which were expressly referred to in a contract, even though the defendant had not seen those terms, and the absence of an express reference to the jurisdiction clause (*7E Communications Ltd v Vertex Antennentechnik GmbH* [2007] EWCA Civ 140, [2008] Bus LR 472).

On the principle of the severability of a jurisdiction clause, see *Deutsche Bank AG v Asia Pacific Broadband Wireless Communications Inc.* [2008] EWHC 918 (Comm), LTL 7/5/2008.

Tort

16.30 **Meaning of 'tort'**   A contribution claim under the Civil Liability (Contribution) Act 1978, s. 1 (see **29.2**) comes within the Jurisdiction and Judgments Regulation, art. 5(3) (*Hewden Tower Cranes Ltd v Wolffkran GmbH* [2007] EWHC 857 (TCC), [2007] 2 Lloyd's Rep 138).

Trusts

16.34 The terms 'settlor, trustee or beneficiary' in the Jurisdiction and Judgments Regulation, art. 5(6), have to be construed restrictively. Accordingly, a person with power to appoint who would take the assets under a trust (but who was not a named trustee) was not a trustee under art. 5(6), and a person who the claimant alleged had been wrongly given trust assets was not a 'beneficiary' (*Gómez v Encarnación Gómez-Monche Vives* [2008] EWHC 259 (Ch), [2008] 3 WLR 309).

Co-defendants

16.36 Claims may be connected for the purposes of the Jurisdiction and Judgments Regulation, art. 6(1), even if they have different legal bases (such as contract and tort) (*Freeport plc v Arnoldsson* (case C-98/06) [2008] QB 634). Further, provided the conditions of art. 6(1) are satisfied, there is no need for the claimant to establish that the claims have not been brought for the sole purpose of ousting the jurisdiction of the courts where any of the defendants are domiciled.

Alternative or contingent claims were regarded as falling within art. 6(1) in *FKI Engineering Ltd v De Wind Holdings Ltd* [2008] EWCA Civ 316, LTL 28/2/2008.

Lis pendens

16.38 The parties may be 'the same' within the meaning of the Jurisdiction and Judgments Regulation, art. 27(1), even if they were separate legal persons, provided there was a sufficient degree of identity between them. This might arise where a judgment against one would amount to *res judicata* against the other, or where the parties have identical interests (*Kolden Holdings Ltd v Rodette Commerce Ltd* [2008] EWCA Civ 10, [2008] Bus LR 1051).

16.39 **Court first seised**   To come within the Jurisdiction and Judgment Regulation, art. 30(2), a document has to be capable of being served and lodged with the court so as to institute proceedings. A writ lodged without a translation as required by local court rules performed this function in *WPP Holdings Italy SRL v Benatti* [2007] EWCA Civ 263, [2007] 1 WLR 2316.

Related actions

16.40 Article 28 of the Jurisdiction and Judgments Regulation, in talking about the 'risk' of irreconcilable judgments, gives the court room to say the connection between two claims is not sufficiently close, or the risk of irreconcilable judgments insufficiently great, to make the actions 'related' within art. 28 (*Research in Motion UK Ltd v Visto Corporation* [2008] EWCA Civ 153, [2008] FSR 20).

ASSUMED JURISDICTION

Procedure on seeking permission

A failure to include a statement of the ground on which the claimant alleges he is entitled **16.45** to serve a claim outside the jurisdiction in the claim form is an irregularity, which will be corrected under CPR, r. 3.10, in the absence of prejudice to the defendant (*Harris Calnan Construction Co. Ltd v Ridgewood (Kensington) Ltd* [2007] EWHC 2738 (TCC), [2008] Bus LR 636).

Grounds for granting permission

General interpretation   *Metall und Rohstoff AG v Donaldson Lufkin and Jenrette Inc.* [1990] **16.46** 1 QB 391, which held that the specific ground under what is now PD6B, para. 3.1, must be stated in the pleading or witness statement in support of the application for permission to serve outside the jurisdiction, was followed in *E. D. and F. Man Sugar Ltd v Lendoudis* [2007] EWHC 2268 (Comm), [2008] 1 All ER 952. In this case it was held that the rule cannot be evaded by reliance on the principle that it is sufficient to plead the materials facts, and that there is no need to state the legal result (*Re Vandervell's Trusts (No. 2)* [1974] Ch 269).

There is no power under PD6B, para. 3.1, to grant permission for service outside the jurisdiction of orders requiring officers of a company to attend court or to produce documents pursuant to r. 71.2 (*Vitol SA v Capri Marine Ltd* [2008] EWHC 378 (Comm), LTL 7/3/ 2008).

Contract   A claim under the Civil Liability (Contribution) Act 1978, s. 1 (see **29.2**), comes **16.50** within PD6B, para. 3.1(6), as a claim 'in respect of a contract' even though the claimant is not a party to that contract (*Greene Wood and McLean v Templeton Insurance Ltd* [2008] EWHC 1593 (Comm), LTL 17/7/2008). A claim to enforce a trust which arose from a contract is also a claim in respect of a contract within r. 6.20(5) (*Cherney v Deripaska* [2008] EWHC 1530 (Comm), LTL 8/7/2008).

Tort   Economic loss in England following an accident in Australia was sufficient for the **16.51** purposes of PD6B, para. 3.1(9)(a), (*Cooley v Ramsey* [2008] EWHC 129 (QB), LTL 11/3/2008).

The proper place to bring the claim (*forum conveniens*)

England was the forum where a claim could be most suitably tried, despite Russia being the **16.54** natural forum, when there were risks that the claimant would be arrested on trumped up charges and would not get a fair trial of his claim (*Cherney v Deripaska* [2008] EWHC 1530 (Comm), LTL 8/7/2008).

INJUNCTIONS TO RESTRAIN FOREIGN PROCEEDINGS

An anti-suit injunction is an interim or ancillary order, not a substantive cause of action **16.72** requiring a separate basis establishing jurisdiction (*Masri v Consolidated Contractors International Co. SAL* [2008] EWCA Civ 625, *The Times*, 25 June 2008).

Chapter 17   Admitting the Claim and Requesting Time to Pay

WITHDRAWAL OF AN ADMISSION

In *Telling v OCS Group Ltd* (2008) LTL 2/6/2008 (Sheffield County Court) it was held there had been a **17.4** binding agreement that the defendant would not withdraw an admission of liability in consideration of the claimant ending her investigations into the accident. In *Green v Brunel and Family Housing Association* (2008) LTL 6/6/2008 (Bradford County Court) the judge struck out sections of a defence which sought to resile from pre-action admissions. A distinction was drawn between fast track claims (where the Pre-action Protocol for Personal Injury Claims creates a presumption that such admissions will be binding) and multi-track claims. This was a fast track case, and the claimant would have suffered prejudice if the admissions were withdrawn.

Chapter 19   Disputing the Court's Jurisdiction

INTRODUCTION

19.1   CPR, Part 11, is not limited to cases where the dispute is about territorial jurisdiction. It also applies to disputes over the court's power or authority to try a claim, such as where there is an arbitration clause or where a claim form is served after it has expired (*Hoddinott v Persimmon Homes (Wessex) Ltd* [2007] EWCA Civ 1203, [2008] 1 WLR 806).

SUBMISSION TO JURISDICTION

19.4   Participation by a property holder as an applicant in interpleader proceedings does not ordinarily amount to a submission to the jurisdiction because the purpose is to gain the protection of the court from the competing claimants (*Australia v Peacekeeper International FZC UAE* [2008] EWHC 1220 (QB), LTL 9/6/2008).

Chapter 20   Default Judgment

Where the default judgment was not entered wrongly

20.13   If the investigations for the evidence required for an application to set aside are not straightforward, such as where evidence has to be sought from a distant country, an application may be prompt within the meaning of CPR, r. 13.3(2), even if it is issued several weeks after the default judgment (*Shandong Chenming Paper Holding Ltd v Saga Forest Carriers Intl AS* [2008] EWHC 1055 (Comm), LTL 16/5/2008).

Discretion to set aside

20.16   There was a real prospect of success in establishing a time-bar defence where there was some documentary evidence in support of an argument that the cause of action accrued just outside the relevant time limit (*Shandong Chenming Paper Holding Ltd v Saga Forest Carriers Intl AS* [2008] EWHC 1055 (Comm), LTL 16/5/2008).

Setting aside on conditions

20.19   The *M. V. Yorke Motors v Edwards* [1982] 1 WLR 444 principles in dealing with allegations of want of means are applied across other areas of civil procedure, and are not restricted to conditions for setting aside default judgments (*El Nasharty v J. Sainsbury plc* [2007] EWHC 2618 (Comm), [2008] 1 Lloyd's Rep 360 (application for stay in favour of arbitration)).

Chapter 23   Claim Form

INTRODUCTION

The term 'statement of case' within CPR, r. 2.3, extends to the acknowledgment of service **23.1** and detailed grounds for contesting a claim for judicial review (*R (Corner House Research) v Director of the Serious Fraud Office* [2008] EWHC 246 (Admin), [2008] 3 WLR 568).

STATEMENT OF TRUTH

Liability for a statement of truth

Settling the claim does not remove the jurisdiction to bring proceedings for contempt of **23.13** court in respect of documents verified by allegedly false statements of truth (*Kirk v Walton* [2008] EWHC 1780 (QB), LTL 31/7/2008). Permission to bring contempt of court proceedings was granted in *Kirk v Walton* where the evidence verified by the statements of truth had been persisted in over a prolonged period of time, the contrary evidence raised a strong prima facie case of falsity such that the applicant's arguments could not be regarded as either tenuous or argumentative.

Consequence of failure to verify a statement of case

The usual order on failing to verify a statement of case is to allow the defaulting **23.17** party a limited period of time to file a verified statement of case. Setting aside an order granting permission to serve outside the jurisdiction on the ground that the claim form and witness statement were not signed was regarded as disproportionate in *Colliers International Property Consultants v Colliers Jordan Lee Jafaar Sdn Bhd* [2008] EWHC 1524 (Comm), LTL 10/7/2008.

OTHER MATTERS TO BE SET OUT IN THE CLAIM FORM

For claim forms to be served outside the jurisdiction, PD 7, paras 3.5 and 3.5A, are replaced **23.18** by a new para. 3.5 with effect from 1 October 2008. This provides that where a claim form to be served out of the jurisdiction is one which the court has power to deal with under the Civil Jurisdiction and Judgments Act 1982 and the Jurisdiction and Judgments Regulation, the claim form must, pursuant to CPR, r. 6.34, be filed and served with form N510 (see PD 6B, para. 2.1).

Chapter 24   Particulars of Claim

STRUCTURE OF PARTICULARS OF CLAIM

Breach of duty

While the court will be slow to strike out for failing to give sufficient particulars of negligence, **24.12** where the claimant has been given the opportunity to provide those particulars and fails to do so, striking out may be appropriate (*S v Chapman* [2008] EWCA Civ 800, LTL 20/5/2008).

Other relevant matters

24.14 Particulars of claim should include the names of persons who play a significant part in the narrative relating to the claim (such as persons to whom a libel is alleged to have been published) (*Freer v Zeb* [2008] EWHC 212 (QB), LTL 21/2/2008).

Allegations of abuse of process and anti-suit injunctions

24.16A Any allegation of abuse of process should be fully pleaded in the statements of case so that the true nature of the issue can be identified and considered in advance of the trial (*Conlon v Simms* [2006] EWCA Civ 1749, [2008] 1 WLR 484, at [151], [166] and [176]). There is probably a similar obligation to plead any claim for an anti-suit injunction in the particulars of claim (*Albon v Naza Motor Trading Sdn Bhd (No. 4)* [2007] EWCA Civ 1124, [2008] 1 All ER (Comm) 351, at [9]).

It is necessary for allegations of fraud to be separately and distinctly pleaded in order to comply with CPR, r. 16.2(1)(a) (*Berezovsky v Abramovich* [2008] EWHC 1138 (Comm), LTL 30/5/2008).

UNPLEADED ALLEGATIONS

24.24 While a court should give a fair reading to a pleading, it was not open to the court below in *Lawrence v Poorah* [2008] UKPC 21, LTL 9/4/2008, to read allegations of undue influence or unconscionable bargain into an imprecisely drawn statement of case. There are limits on the degree to which a judge can intervene, even with the scope of the active case management powers granted by CPR, Part 1, in defining a case for a party. Ultimately, the judge must remain scrupulously impartial, and it is wrong to conclude, while giving judgment, that the claimant should succeed on an unpleaded basis. An appeal against a decision on an unpleaded basis may be dismissed if there is no real injustice in that the evidence would be the same on the new basis of the claim (*Whitecap Leisure Ltd v John H. Rundle Ltd* [2008] EWCA Civ 429, [2008] 2 Lloyd's Rep 216).

Chapter 25   Schedules of Special Damages

INTRODUCTION

25.1 In *Tomer v Atlantic Cleaning Service Ltd* [2008] EWHC 1652 (QB), LTL 25/7/2008, particulars of claim which stated that a schedule of past and future loss and expense was 'to follow' were held to include a claim for special damages (which could accordingly be attacked by way of striking out or a request for further information).

Chapter 29   Additional Claims under Part 20

CONTRIBUTION

29.2 A claim in breach of trust or fiduciary duty is a claim for compensation in respect of any damage within the meaning of the Civil Liability (Contribution) Act 1978, ss. 1(1) and 6(1), if it is a claim to make good the claimant's loss, whereas a claim for an account of profits falls outside the statute (*Charter plc v City Index Ltd* [2007] EWCA Civ 1382, [2008] Ch 313).

In *Charter plc v City Index Ltd* a claim that a company's auditors and directors had allowed unauthorised transactions to continue in breach of duty to the company was held to be in respect of the same damage as a claim in breach of trust or fiduciary duty against a manager who used the company's funds to finance his personal betting transactions. Permission to appeal to the House of Lords has been granted ([2008] 1 WLR 1334).

A contribution could be claimed under s. 1(1) from the company in fact liable to a former employee where a residuary body mistakenly paid compensation to the former employee (*BRB (Residuary) Ltd v Connex South Eastern Ltd* [2008] EWHC 1172 (QB), LTL 30/5/2008).

PROCEDURE FOR FILING AN ADDITIONAL CLAIM WHERE PERMISSION IS REQUIRED

Relevant considerations in applications for permissions to file an additional claim

29.7 Being a discretionary decision, an appeal court can only interfere with a decision on permission to file an additional claim where the judge either fails to apply the correct principles or makes a decision outside the generous ambit of the discretion (*Walbrook Trustees (Jersey) Ltd v Fattal* [2008] EWCA Civ 427, LTL 11/3/2008).

Chapter 30   Further Information

REQUEST FOR FURTHER INFORMATION

30.2 It is unusual in patent infringement claims for the court to order a party to answer a request for further information to clarify the construction they proposed to put on the terms of the patent (*Lux Traffic Controls Ltd v Staffordshire Public Works* [1991] RPC 73). This is not an invariable rule, and it may save costs to order further information where the answers will assist in defining the issues before experts are instructed (*Novartis AG v Johnson and Johnson Medical Ltd* [2008] EWHC 293 (Pat), LTL 5/3/2008).

Harcourt v Griffin [2007] EWHC 1500 (QB), [2007] PIQR Q177, was not followed in *West London Pipeline and Storage Ltd v Total UK Ltd* [2008] EWHC 1296 (Comm), LTL 11/6/2008, where it was held there is no jurisdiction to order a party to disclose its insurance position, because this is not a matter in dispute in the proceedings.

Chapter 31   Amendments to Statements of Case

PRINCIPLES ON WHICH PERMISSION IS GRANTED

31.4 The *Clarapede* principles were applied in *Scobie v Fairview Land Ltd* [2008] EWHC 147 (TCC), LTL 11/2/2008.

Despite *La Chemise Lacoste SA v Sketchers USA Ltd* [2006] EWHC 3642 (Ch), LTL 24/5/2006, the normal rule is that the applicant should pay the costs of the application to amend (*Lidl UK GmbH v Davies* [2008] EWCA Civ 976, LTL 10/7/2008).

Amendments with no real prospect of success

31.6 In *Multiplex Construction (UK) Ltd v Cleveland Bridge UK Ltd* [2008] EWHC 231 (TCC), LTL 9/5/2008, the court refused permission to make amendments which were regarded as being incomprehensible.

AMENDMENT AFTER A RELEVANT LIMITATION PERIOD HAS EXPIRED

New cause of action

31.17 In *Evans v Cig Mon Cymru Ltd* [2008] EWCA Civ 390, [2008] PIQR P17, the claimant had contemplated bringing claims against his former employer for damages following an accident at work, and a claim based on workplace bullying. He decided to pursue only the personal injury claim, and issued a claim form shortly before the expiry of limitation. After limitation it was noticed that the claim form described the claim as for 'loss and damage arising out of abuse at work'. The supporting medical report and particulars of claim were based on the accident. It was held to be permissible to read the claim form together with the particulars of claim and medical report to determine what the claim was intended to cover. In context, the words 'of abuse' were an obvious clerical error for the phrase 'of an accident', and permission to amend was granted as the amendment did not involve introducing a new claim within the meaning of CPR, r. 17.4.

Same or substantially the same facts

31.19 **Raised by either party** The *Goode v Martin* [2001] EWCA Civ 1899, [2002] 1 WLR 1828, principle was applied by the Court of Appeal in *Lidl UK GmbH v Davies* [2008] EWCA Civ 976, LTL 10/7/2008.

Chapter 32   Applications and Interim Orders

APPLICATIONS WITH NOTICE

Standard of proof on disputed facts on interim applications

32.15 The 'good arguable case' test was applied in a dispute as to whether the parties were 'the same' for the purposes of the Jurisdiction and Judgments Regulation, reg. 27, in *Kolden Holdings Ltd v Rodette Commerce Ltd* [2008] EWCA Civ 10, [2008] Bus LR 1051. It was also applied to a disputed condition under the Jurisdiction and Judgments regulation in *Crucial Music Corporation v Klondyke Management AG* [2007] EWHC 1782 (Ch), [2008] Bus LR 327. It is intended to encapsulate the critical rule that the court must be as satisfied as it can be, given the limitations of an interim application, that factors existed which gave the court jurisdiction. Inevitably, the way the test is applied must vary from case to case (*WPP Holdings Italy SRL v Benatti* [2007] EWCA Civ 263, [2007] 1 WLR 2316).

GENERAL POWERS REGARDING INTERIM RELIEF AND ORDERS

32.30 The High Court has power under the Civil Jurisdiction and Judgments Act 1982, s. 25(1), to grant interim relief where proceedings have been or are to be commenced in another jurisdiction. This is discussed in relation to freezing injunctions at **38.6**. The principle underpinning s. 25 is that the High Court should be willing to assist the courts of other jurisdictions by providing interim relief on the same basis as if the High Court was itself seised of the substantive claim (*Kensington International Ltd v Republic of Congo* [2007] EWCA Civ 1128, [2008] 1 WLR 1144).

Chapter 33   Striking Out

GENERAL TEST

The test on striking out is the same even where one party is suffering from an inequality of **33.6** arms (*Bank of Tokyo-Mitsubishi UFJ Ltd v Baskan Gida Sanayi ve Pazarlama AS* [2008] EWHC 659 (Ch), LTL 17/4/2008).

NO REASONABLE GROUNDS FOR BRINGING OR DEFENDING THE CLAIM

In *Freer v Zeb* [2008] EWHC 212 (QB), LTL 21/2/2008, a claim that the defendant was vicariously **33.7** liable for other persons' actions, as their employer, was struck out, because all the evidence was that the persons were not employed by the defendant but by a company of which the defendant was a director.

ABUSE OF PROCESS

General examples of abuse of process

Participation in a fraudulent claim, while a serious breach of the overriding objective, did not **33.13** render the separate claim by the claimant an abuse justifying striking out in *Ul-Haq v Shah* [2008] EWHC 1896 (QB), LTL 11/8/2008 (where indemnity basis costs were awarded against the participant in the fraud).

While it is an abuse of process to start proceedings with no intention to progress them to trial, protracted delay combined with a legitimate concern to avoid costs in the hope of settlement do not amount to this (*Artibell Shipping Co. Ltd v Markel International Insurance Co. Ltd* [2008] EWHC 811 (Comm), LTL 2/5/2008).

Relitigation as an abuse of process

Generally it is an abuse of process to have simultaneously two active, identical, claims against **33.14** the same defendant. This is because it is oppressive to force a defendant into defending the same claim in multiple proceedings. A claim is active for this purpose once it is served, and it is a common precaution where there is a technical problem with proceedings to issue a second, protective, claim (which is not served) pending resolution of the objections to the first claim. In *Rosenberg v Nazarov* [2008] EWHC 812 (Ch), LTL 10/4/2008, there were two active claims against the defendant, the only difference between the two particulars of claim being two paragraphs. The court declined to strike out the first claim because it was issued eight months before the second, and there were potential limitation problems with the second claim which would not affect the first, and the court took the view that consolidation would avoid any oppression to the defendant.

Issue which should have been raised in earlier proceedings   *WWF-World Wide Fund for Nature* **33.16** *v World Wrestling Federation Entertainment Inc.* [2007] EWCA Civ 286 is reported at [2008] 1 WLR 445.

The effect of the rule in *Hollington v F. Hewthorn and Co. Ltd* [1943] 1 KB 587 (see **47.94** and **47.99**) is that previous findings from cases involving different parties are inadmissible as evidence of the facts on which those findings were based. What *Secretary of State for Trade and Industry v Bairstow* [2003] EWCA Civ 321, [2004] Ch 1, does is to provide a means of circumventing that rule on the theory that, if an abuse of process is established, the party against whom the previous finding was made is prevented from asserting facts contrary to the previous finding (*Conlon v Simms* [2006] EWCA Civ 1749, [2008] 1 WLR 484, at [177], per Ward LJ). In applying the principles in *Secretary of State for Trade and Industry v Bairstow* the court should be slower in preventing a party from continuing to deny serious charges after a previous adverse finding by way of defence, than in preventing a party from initiating proceedings for the purpose of launching a collateral attack on such a previous finding (*Conlon v Simms*). In *Conlon v Simms* the court refused to strike out a solicitor's defence in a claim by the solicitor's former partners which alleged they had been induced to enter into partnership with him by fraudulent misrepresentations. It would have been unfair to allow the claimant to raise findings of the Solicitors Disciplinary Tribunal in previous disciplinary proceedings against the solicitor without having to prove its case, which would have been the position if the defence had been struck out as an abuse of process.

Chapter 34   Summary Judgment

INTRODUCTION

34.1   Many applications under the Companies Acts are made on a summary basis, usually on the hearing of the substantive Part 8 claim. It is also possible for these applications to be made by way of summary judgment applications (*Oxford Legal Group Ltd v Sibbasbridge Services plc* [2008] EWCA Civ 387, *The Times*, 15 May 2008).

TEST FOR ENTERING SUMMARY JUDGMENT

34.10   In *Bee v Jenson* [2006] EWHC 2534 (Comm), [2007] RTR 9, the court adopted the approach explained by Potter LJ in *E. D. and F. Man Liquid Products Ltd v Patel* [2003] EWCA Civ 472, [2003] CPLR 384 at [8]: 'I regard the distinction between a realistic and fanciful prospect of success as appropriately reflecting the observation in the *Saudi Eagle* that the defence sought to be argued must carry some degree of conviction. Both approaches require the defendant to have a case which is better than merely arguable, as was formerly the case under RSC, ord. 14.'

Where the respondent's evidence, taken at its highest, does not raise a possibility of a defence, but is in the realm of a mere (and distinctly improbable) possibility, it is right to enter summary judgment (*Akinleye v East Sussex Hospitals NHS Trust* [2008] EWHC 68 (QB), [2008] LS Law Med 216). So, where the respondent's assertion that he retained a beneficial interest in property was unsupported by documentary evidence and where the circumstances (such as no provision for any rental income or how his interest was to be realised) were regarded as fantastic, summary judgment was entered (*Sandhar v Sandhar and Kang Ltd* [2008] EWCA Civ 238, LTL 14/2/2008). Conversely, where there is some prospect of success, summary judgement should be refused, and the court should not conduct a mini-trial into disputed questions of fact (*Cotton v Rickard Metals Inc.* [2008] EWHC 824 (QB), LTL 25/4/2008).

The test for summary judgment is the same even where one party is suffering from an inequality of arms (*Bank of Tokyo-Mitsubishi UFJ Ltd v Baskan Gida Sanayi ve Pazarlama AS* [2008] EWHC 659 (Ch), LTL 17/4/2008).

Complex claims

Summary judgment was refused in *Apvodedo NV v Collins* [2008] EWHC 775 (Ch), LTL 29/4/2008, **34.12**
where the respondent raised a defence of common mistake which turned on a detailed
analysis of a complex factual matrix.

Disputes of fact

Where there is no dispute of fact, in that the evidence on liability was either admitted or was **34.15**
derived from matters adduced by the respondent, summary judgment may be entered
(*Wrexham Association Football Club Ltd v Crucialmove Ltd* [2006] EWCA Civ 237, [2008] 1 BCLC 508).
There is no rule that summary judgment is not available where this involves a finding adverse
to the integrity of the respondent (*Wrexham Association Football Club Ltd v Crucialmove Ltd*, where
summary judgment was entered in a claim based on a director being in breach of his duty of
good faith to his company).

Evidence not yet investigated

Where the contractual position between the parties needs to be investigated, and disclosure **34.20**
has not taken place, summary judgement should be refused (*Groveholt Ltd v Hughes* [2008]
EWHC 1358 (Ch), LTL 27/6/2008).

Amendment

It is inappropriate to subject a pleading to too close a syntactical analysis on an application **34.24**
for summary judgement where it is clear on the pleadings overall what the real issues are, and
where any defects in the respondent's pleaded case can be saved by amendment (*Landfast
(Anglia) Ltd v Cameron Taylor One Ltd* [2008] EWHC 343 (TCC), LTL 23/5/2008).

Chapter 35   Possession Claims against Trespassers

If the criteria laid down in *Secretary of State for the Environment, Food and Rural Affairs v Drury*
[2004] EWCA Civ 200, [2004] 1 WLR 1906, are satisfied, the court has a discretion, rather than a
duty, to make an order granting possession of other named sites where the trespassers might
move to. The discretion to refuse such an order should only be exercised in exceptional
circumstances (*Secretary of State for the Environment, Food and Rural Affairs v Meier* [2008] EWCA
Civ 903, LTL 31/7/2008, where an injunction to restrain the defendant from entering or
occupying those sites was also granted).

Chapter 36   Interim Payments

PROCEDURE

Application and evidence

A certificate of benefits must be obtained by the defendant (with effect from 1 October 2008) **36.6**
both in personal injuries claims and claims in which damages in respect of a disease for which
a lump-sum payment within the definition of the Social Security (Recovery of Benefits) Act
1997, s. 1A(2), has been, or is likely to be made.

AMOUNT TO BE ORDERED

36.15 A 'reasonable proportion of the likely amount of the final judgment' within the meaning of CPR, r. 25.7(4), in a personal injuries claim is not limited to the likely lump-sum award, but also includes the capitalised value of any likely award for periodical payments (*Braithwaite v Homerton University Hospitals NHS Foundation Trust* [2008] EWHC 353 (QB), [2008] LS Law Med 261). In deciding how much to order by way of interim payment in a personal injuries claim where the claimant had suffered catastrophic injuries, the court in *Mealing v Chelsea and Westminster NHS Trust* [2007] EWHC 3254 (QB), [2008] LS Law Med 236, took into account:

(a) whether there was any likelihood that the amount ordered would pre-empt any decision by the trial judge on any of the issues between the parties;

(b) that ordering too much by way of interim payments could act as a disincentive to the claimant in progressing the claim to trial; and

(c) that if too much were ordered by way of interim payments, the amount left to be awarded at trial might be too little to make an effective periodical payments order, or too little to make an effective lump-sum award for the necessary capital expenses for the claimant's care.

There is a standard interim payment for mesothelioma claims (PD 3D), which is currently £50,000 (47th Update).

PD 40B, paras 5.1 and 5.1A, add further detail to the form of interim payment orders where there are recoverable benefits or lump-sum awards affected by the Social Security (Recovery of Benefits) Act 1997 (47th Update, with effect from 1 October 2008). See also **61.19** in this supplement.

Chapter 37   Interim Injunctions

SUBSTANTIVE CAUSE OF ACTION

37.15 *Kensington International Ltd v Republic of Congo* [2007] EWCA Civ 1128 is reported at [2008] 1 WLR 1144.

Person unknown as defendant

37.17 PD 7, paras 3.5 and 3.5A, have been reworded and no longer use the word 'should'.

EXCEPTIONAL CASES

Final disposal of the claim

37.34 The 'high degree of assurance' test (the usual test for interim mandatory injunctions, see 37.50) was applied in the final disposal case of *Chambers v British Olympic Association* [2008] EWHC 2028 (QB), LTL 18/7/2008.

Copyright, privacy and confidentiality claims

37.37 *Murray v Big Pictures (UK) Ltd* [2008] EWCA Civ 446, [2008] EMLR 12, overturned the decision at first instance (*Murray v Express Newspapers plc* [2007] EWHC 1908 (Ch), [2007] EMLR 22), and held that, subject to the facts of individual cases, an injunction could be granted to restrain publication of photographs of a child even though they were taken in a public place. In deciding whether there has been an infringement of the European Convention on Human

Rights, art. 8, in the Human Rights Act 1998, sch. 1, the first stage is to consider whether there was a reasonable expectation of privacy. Factors to take into account include the attributes of the claimant, what he was doing at the time, where, the nature of the intrusion, whether there was consent, the effect on the claimant and the circumstances of the proposed publication. The second stage is to balance the competing rights under the Convention (frequently arts 8 and 10). At this stage the court takes into account whether the publication would be highly offensive to an objective, reasonable person.

In *Mosley v News Group Newspapers Ltd* [2008] EWHC 1777 (QB), *The Times*, 30 July 2008, it was held that the clandestine recording of sexual activity on private property engages art. 8, and there has to be a particularly serious reason before the court could interfere with that right by invoking the right of freedom of expression under art. 10.

Restraint of legal proceedings

According to *Glencore International AG v Exeter Shipping Ltd* [2002] EWCA Civ 528, [2002] 2 All ER   **37.47**
(Comm) 1, at [42] to [43], the principles applicable when deciding whether an injunction to restrain foreign proceedings should be granted are:

(a) whether the defendant is amenable to the English territorial and personal jurisdiction;
(b) whether it is just and convenient to grant the injunction under the Supreme Court Act 1981, s. 37(1);
(c) in exercising the discretion factors the court will consider include:
    (i) whether the threatened conduct is unconscionable, which primarily refers to conduct which is oppressive, vexatious or unconscionable, or which interferes with the due process of the court;
    (ii) whether injunctive relief is necessary to protect the applicant's legitimate interest in proceedings in England;
    (iii) whether England is the natural forum for the litigation.

The same principles were applied on an application to restrain arbitration proceedings in *Albon v Naza Motor Trading Sdn Bhd (No. 4)* [2007] EWCA Civ 1124, [2008] 1 All ER (Comm) 351. In applying these principles in an arbitration case, Jackson J in *J. Jarvis and Sons Ltd v Blue Circle Dartford Estates Ltd* [2007] EWHC 1262 (TCC), [2007] BLR 439, made the following points, at [40]:

(a) the discretion to grant such an injunction is exercised very sparingly and with due regard to the principles on which the Arbitration Act 1996 is expressly based (for which, see **69.1**); and
(b) delay by the applicant is material to the court's exercise of its discretion, and in some cases will be fatal to the application.

INTERIM MANDATORY INJUNCTIONS

An interim mandatory injunction for the delivery up of an aircraft to its owner was granted in   **37.50**
Shilmore Enterprises Corporation v Phoenix 1 Aviation Ltd [2008] EWHC 169 (QB), LTL 19/2/2008. The court felt a high degree of assurance over the merits of the claim, and was of the view that returning the aircraft to the claimant (who was able to give an effective undertaking in damages) ran the least risk of injustice over the defendant's solution of ordering the aircraft into the joint custody of the parties and preventing it from being flown.

UNDERTAKINGS GIVEN BY THE DEFENDANT

Where undertakings are given by a defendant and incorporated into a consent order, the   **37.59**
undertakings may be construed as having contractual effect between the parties. In such a case

breach of the undertakings may be enforced as breaches of contract, resulting in a claim for damages (*Independiente Ltd v Music Trading On-Line (HK) Ltd* [2007] EWCA Civ 111, [2008] 1 WLR 608).

Chapter 38   Freezing Injunctions

CONDITIONS FOR GRANTING FREEZING INJUNCTIONS

Claim justiciable in England and Wales

38.5 An application to the court for a freezing injunction in support of arbitration proceedings under the Arbitration Act 1996, s. 44, has the advantages that the court's order will bind third parties and is buttressed by sanctions (*Pacific Maritime (Asia) Ltd v Holystone Overseas Ltd* [2007] EWHC 2319 (Comm), [2008] 1 Lloyd's Rep 371).

Injunctions in support of foreign proceedings

38.6 ICSID arbitration proceedings are not 'proceedings' for the purpose of the Civil Jurisdiction and Judgments Act 1982, s. 25. This is because the power in s. 25(3)(c), to extend s. 25 to arbitration proceedings was repealed by the Arbitration Act 1996, and while the Arbitration Act 1996 contains a power to extend the Arbitration Act 1996, s. 44, no such order has been made for ICSID arbitration proceedings (*ETI Euro Telecom International NV v Bolivia* [2008] EWCA Civ 880, LTL 28/7/2008). Further, the foreign proceedings have to be on the substance of the dispute, so foreign attachment proceedings, being interim in nature, do not come within s. 25 (*ETI Euro Telecom International NV v Bolivia*).

Worldwide freezing injunctions

38.9 The power to grant worldwide freezing injunctions in support of domestic proceedings derives from the Supreme Court Act 1981, s. 37(1), not the Civil Jurisdiction and Judgments Act 1992, s. 25 (*Masri v Consolidated Contractors International UK Ltd (No. 2)* [2007] EWHC 3030 (Comm), [2008] 1 All ER (Comm) 305, at [53], at first instance; see, on appeal, [2008] EWCA Civ 303, [2008] 2 Lloyd's Rep 128). The same applies to worldwide freezing injunctions in support of domestic judgments (*Masri v Consolidated Contractors International UK Ltd (No. 2)*, at first instance, at [58]). A worldwide freezing injunction in aid of foreign proceedings will only be granted where the respondent or the dispute has a sufficiently strong link with the jurisdiction, or if there is some other factor justifying the court's intervention despite the lack of such a link (*Mobil Cerro Negro Ltd v Petróleos de Venezuela SA* [2008] EWHC 532 (Comm), [2008] 1 Lloyd's Rep 684).

Risk of disposal

38.12 There has to be 'solid evidence' of the risk of disposal (*Ninemia Maritime Corp v Trave Schiffahrts GmbH and Co. KG* [1983] 1 WLR 1412; *Dean and Dean v Grinina* [2008] EWHC 927 (QB), LTL 13/5/2008).

38.13 **Assessing risk**   It is not every case where there are allegations of negligence, breach of contract and breach of fiduciary duty that it is appropriate to infer risk of disposal of assets from the nature of the allegation in the substantive cause of action (*Renewable Power and Light plc v Renewable Power and Light Services Inc.* [2008] EWHC 1058 (Ch), LTL 23/5/2008).

CONTENTS OF A FREEZING INJUNCTION

Undertakings

38.15 In the event that the order is discharged, the defendant is entitled to both special and general damages arising from the effects of the order. Special damages might include disruption to the defendant's business and management time in dealing with the order. The scale of the order (particularly if combined with a search order) may of itself be sufficient for the court to be satisfied that there was significant disruption to the defendant's business (*Aerospace Publishing Ltd v Thames Water Utilities Ltd* [2007] EWCA Civ 3, [2007] Bus LR 726; *Al-Rawas v Pegasus Energy Ltd* [2008] EWHC 617 (QB), LTL 16/4/2008). In most circumstances evidence is required to support an award for general damages; damages for emotional distress are not recoverable; and exemplary damages are unlikely to be appropriate (*Al-Rawas v Pegasus Energy Ltd*).

Assets covered by the order

38.17 A maximum-sum order should freeze the highest amount, including interest and costs, for which the claimant has a good arguable case (*Pacific Maritime (Asia) Ltd v Holystone Overseas Ltd* [2007] EWHC 2319 (Comm), [2008] 1 Lloyd's Rep 371).

Costs of litigation

38.24 The standard litigation costs clause in a freezing injunction does not cover the costs of unnecessary legal advice (*Chantrey Vellacott v Convergence Group plc* (2008) LTL 23/6/2008).

Disclosure of assets orders

38.25 An assets disclosure order can be granted under CPR, r. 25.1(1)(g), where there is a reasonable possibility, based on credible evidence, that a freezing injunction application might be made (*Lichter v Rubin* [2008] EWHC 450 (Ch), *The Times*, 18 April 2008). While there is no free-standing power to grant this type of order, they can be made where there is a likelihood of a freezing injunction application (*Parker v CS Structured Credit Fund Ltd* [2003] EWHC 391 (Ch), [2003] 1 WLR 1680).

Cross-examination as to assets

38.27 Where a third party is to be cross-examined as to the assets of a defendant, it is likely to be appropriate to require the claimant to give a cross-undertaking not to use the answers for collateral purposes. In *Dadourian Group International v Simms* [2008] EWHC 186 (Ch), LTL 19/5/2008, an undertaking not to use the answers for the purposes of 'any criminal or committal proceedings, or for the trial of the actions' was held to cover use in a summary judgment application. Similar considerations to those laid down in *Dadourian Group International v Simms (No. 2)* [2006] EWCA Civ 1745, [2007] 1 WLR 2967 (see **38.10**) were applied in deciding whether to release the claimant from this undertaking. It was also held that two defendants had no standing to object to the lifting of the undertaking as it was given to protect the third party, not them.

VARIATION OR DISCHARGE OF A FREEZING INJUNCTION

Discharge on the basis of material non-disclosure

38.35 'Trap' applications for freezing injunctions, where a buyer obtains a without notice freezing injunction shortly before executing a contract (so the seller in effect walks into a trap when executing the contract), have to be disclosed. If disclosed, the court is unlikely to grant the order. If not disclosed, the court is likely to discharge the order for material non-disclosure (*Swift-Fortune Ltd v Magnifica Marine SA* [2007] EWHC 1630 (Comm), [2008] 1 Lloyd's Rep 54).

Delay in objecting to alleged non-disclosures can be a reason in itself for dismissing an application to discharge (*Indicii Salus Ltd v Chandrasekaran* [2008] EWCA Civ 67, LTL 12/2/2008, a search order case).

FREEZING INJUNCTIONS AFTER JUDGMENT

38.40 Freezing injunctions after judgment, like freezing injunctions in support of pending proceedings, operate *in personam* rather than *in rem* (*Masri v Consolidated Contractors International UK Ltd (No. 2)* [2007] EWHC 3030 (Comm), [2008] 1 All ER (Comm) 305, at [64] to [75]).

Chapter 39   Search Orders

DISCHARGE AND VARIATION OF SEARCH ORDERS

Discharge of search orders

39.18 An appeal was dismissed in *Indicii Salus Ltd v Chandrasekaran* [2008] EWCA Civ 67, LTL 12/2/2008. It was held that the fact the applicant's accountants had reservations about its ability to pay their fees did not have to be disclosed on an application for a search order, and that a statement that an asset had a substantial but uncertain value had not been false.

Chapter 42   Case Management

TRANSFER TO APPROPRIATE COURT

42.3 The High Court has unlimited power under the County Courts Act 1984, s. 40(2), to transfer cases to the county court regardless of whether the case is outside the monetary limits of the county court (*National Westminster Bank plc v King* [2008] EWHC 280 (Ch), [2008] 2 WLR 1279).

An application for a transfer from a county court to a specialist list should be made to the receiving court under CPR, r. 30.5, with notice to the relevant county court (*Collins v Drumgold* [2008] EWHC 584 (TCC), [2008] CILL 2585). A court dealing with an application to transfer a claim from the county court has to consider the matters set out in CPR, r. 30.3(2) (*Lumbermans Mutual Casualty Co. v Bovis Lend Lease Ltd* [2004] EWHC 1614 (Comm), [2004] 2 CLS 778). In considering an application for a transfer to the Technology and Construction Court, Coulson J in *Collins v Drumgold* said the following matters should be considered:

(a) whether the dispute arose out of or was connected with a claim of a type set out in PD 60, para. 2.1;
(b) the value of the claim and its complexity;
(c) the convenience of the parties;
(d) any costs implications in proceeding in the High Court rather than the county court (sometimes transferring to a specialist list will save costs).

Automatic case management orders pilot scheme

42.33 Under PD 51 (47th Update) there is a 12-month pilot scheme for certain case management orders. PD 51 sets up the automatic orders pilot scheme which:

(a) operates from 1 October 2008 to 30 September 2009;

(b) operates in the county courts at Chelmsford, Newcastle, Teesside, Watford and York; and

(c) applies to claims started on or after 1 October 2008.

The automatic orders pilot scheme applies, by para. 1.2, where:

(a) all parties request a stay of proceedings for one month;

(b) any party fails to file an allocation questionnaire; or

(c) there is only one claimant and one defendant, the claim is allocated to the fast track, and a party fails to file a pre-trial checklist.

Further details are contained in PD 51 in the supplement to **appendix 1**.

Chapter 43   Small Claims

EUROPEAN SMALL CLAIMS PROCEDURE

Regulation (EC) No. 861/2007 of 11 July 2007 (the 'ESCP Regulation') establishes a **43.34** European Small Claims Procedure ('ESCP') with effect from 1 January 2009. The Regulation applies, in cross-border cases, to civil and commercial matters, whatever the nature of the court or tribunal, where the value of a claim does not exceed €2,000 at the time when the claim form is received by the court or tribunal with jurisdiction, excluding all interest, expenses and disbursements (art. 2(1)). There are various excepted categories of claim in art. 2(1) and (2). The ESCP is intended to simplify and speed up litigation concerning small claims in cross-border cases, whilst reducing costs, by offering an optional tool in addition to the possibilities existing under the laws of the member States, which will remain unaffected. The ESCP Regulation should also make it simpler to obtain the recognition and enforcement of a judgment given in the ESCP in another member State (recital 8).

There is a special ESCP claim form, which is completed and filed in accordance with the ESCP Regulation, in particular art. 4(1), and which has a declaration which is treated in England and Wales in the same way as a statement of truth (CPR, r. 78.13). ESCP claims are treated as if they were allocated to the small claims track (r. 78.14(1)), and the provisions of Part 27 apply except for r. 27.14 (costs in small claims track cases). There are also detailed procedural rules in the ESCP Regulation so these claims are primarily governed by the ESCP Regulation (PD 78, para. 10). Where the ESCP Regulation is silent, the CPR apply with necessary modifications. In particular, where the ESCP Regulation is silent on service, the Service Regulation and the CPR apply as appropriate (PD 78, para. 15), and CPR, Part 52, applies to any appeals (PD 78, para. 10).

Although there are procedures in the ESCP Regulation for hearings, primarily this is intended to provide a paper-based procedure (art. 5(1)). An oral hearing will only be convened if the court considers this to be necessary or if a party so requests. The decision is ordinarily expected within 30 days of receipt of the response from the defendant (art. 7(1)), although it will be longer if there is an oral hearing. The unsuccessful party must bear the costs of the proceedings. However, the court or tribunal must not award costs to the successful party to the extent that they were unnecessarily incurred or are disproportionate to the claim (art. 16).

Chapter 46   Non-compliance, Sanctions and Relief

PRINCIPLES

Both parties in default

46.9   In *Artibell Shipping Co. Ltd v Markel International Insurance Co. Ltd* [2008] EWHC 811 (Comm), LTL 2/5/2008, there was a two-year delay in fixing a case management conference, but, as it was open to the defendant to do this, striking out the claim was refused.

SANCTIONS

Sanctions available

46.11   The usual order on failing to comply with the CPR or practice directions is to allow the defaulting party a limited period of time to comply, usually with an adverse costs order in respect of any interim application needed to bring the matter before the court (*Colliers International Property Consultants v Colliers Jordan Lee Jafaar Sdn Bhd* [2008] EWHC 1524 (Comm), LTL 10/7/2008 (failure to verify a statement of case)).

STRIKING OUT

Fair trial

46.15   In *Artibell Shipping Co. Ltd v Markel International Insurance Co. Ltd* [2008] EWHC 811 (Comm), LTL 2/5/2008, a fair trial was still possible despite full use of the six-year limitation period, then five years of litigation (including a two-year period in which no progress was made), and a further year to get to trial. Striking out was refused, but security for costs (see **46.19**) was ordered.

EXTENSIONS OF TIME

Rectifying defective performance

46.27   A key factor in deciding whether to set aside or to rectify any irregularity is whether the other side have suffered any prejudice. In the absence of prejudice it is usual to allow the defaulting party to rectify the defect (*Colliers International Property Consultants v Colliers Jordan Lee Jafaar Sdn Bhd* [2008] EWHC 1524 (Comm), LTL 10/7/2008 (failure to serve complete copies of the exhibits with witness statements)).

NON-COMPLIANCE WITH ORDER IMPOSING A SANCTION

46.29   Failing to serve a schedule of special damages within the time stated by an unless order (which specified striking out of the special damages claim in default) resulted in the sanction taking effect automatically (*Tomer v Atlantic Cleaning Service Ltd* [2008] EWHC 1652 (QB), LTL 25/7/2008, applying *Marcan Shipping (London) Ltd v Kefalas* [2007] EWCA Civ 463, [2007] 1 WLR 1864). Technical arguments to avoid this result, such as a purported voluntary withdrawal of the special damages claim, and the fact a schedule had never been served (so there never had been a special damages claim on which the unless order could bite), were rejected.

RELIEF FROM SANCTIONS

Principles governing applications for relief

The courts take into account the problems faced by litigants in person opposed by **46.31**
represented parties in making decisions on sanctions and relief, particularly so where a party
has a serious disability. The question for the court ultimately is whether the disadvantage
under which the party operates explains any default (*Knowles v Knowles* [2008] EWCA Civ 788,
LTL 13/6/2008). The court is entitled to take into account the importance of maintaining the
trial date, and the emphasis placed on this by PD 29, para. 7.4, where problems are caused by
a failure to comply with case management directions (*Ethemi v Shiels* [2008] EWHC 291 (QB), LTL
7/3/2008).

Chapter 47   General Law of Evidence

THE BURDEN AND STANDARD OF PROOF

Standard of proof

For a restatement of the principle that the standard of proof in civil claims is on the balance
of probabilities, see *Re B (Children) (Care Proceedings: Standard of Proof)* [2008] UKHL 35, [2008]
3 WLR 1.

Other cases   Add new point (h):   **47.44**

(h) *Proceeds of crime.* In civil recovery proceedings under the Proceeds of Crime Act 2002,
   part 5, the court must be satisfied to a standard commensurate with the gravity of the case
   (*Director of the Assets Recovery Agency v Virtosu* [2008] EWHC 149 (QB), [2008] 3 All ER 637,
   at [18]).

JUDGMENTS AS EVIDENCE

Previous convictions

Civil Evidence Act 1968, s. 11   If the identical question has already been decided by a   **47.95**
foreign conviction and the foreign judgment contains a summary of the matters proved, that
is admissible as evidence of the truth of those facts in civil proceedings (*Director of the Assets
Recovery Agency v Virtosu* [2008] EWHC 149 (QB), [2008] 3 All ER 637, at [43]).

Other previous findings

Conlon v Simms [2006] EWCA Civ 1749, [2008] 1 WLR 484, reversed the decision at first instance   **47.99**
([2006] EWHC 401 (Ch), [2006] 2 All ER 1024). A solicitor was permitted to deny certain
allegations of dishonest conduct, and it was held that findings against him on those issues by
the Solicitors Disciplinary Tribunal were inadmissible in a later civil claim under the principle
in *Hollington v F. Hewthorn and Co. Ltd* [1943] 1 KB 587. See Jonathan Parker LJ at [135]; Moore-
Bick LJ at [168]; Ward LJ at [177]. See also the discussion of this case at **33.16** in this
supplement on the device of using striking out to achieve a result sidestepping *Hollington v
F. Hewthorn and Co. Ltd*.

Chapter 48   Disclosure

STANDARD DISCLOSURE

Standard disclosure in personal injury claims

48.6   The claimant's medical records will be covered by standard disclosure in a personal injuries claim, almost regardless of the nature of the dispute. The records will either confirm the claimant's injuries and their consequences, or will question those injuries or their extent, and will therefore support either the claimant's or defendant's case (*OCS Group Ltd v Wells* [2008] EWHC 919 (QB), [2008] PIQR P18).

Standard disclosure in professional negligence claims

48.6A   The solicitor's file under the original retainer is almost always, or always, covered by standard disclosure in a solicitors' professional negligence claim (*Martin v Triggs Turner Barton* [2008] EWHC 89 (Ch), *The Times*, 5 February 2008).

MATERIALS TO BE DISCLOSED

Electronic documents

48.10   Disclosure of the metadata behind a record of an important meeting which had been created long after the event was ordered in *Hellard v Money* (2008) LTL 29/4/2008.

DISCLOSURE STATEMENT

Conclusive nature of statements on the status of documents

48.20   The purpose behind the general rule that statements on matters such as the privileged nature of documents withheld from disclosure is the need to avoid mini-trials at the inter-locutory stage (*West London Pipeline and Storage Ltd v Total UK Ltd* [2008] EWHC 1729 (Comm), LTL 23/7/2008). While this is a very strong general rule, it is not absolute, because otherwise a party will be the judge in his own cause, and ultimately claims to privilege have to be proved. Beatson J referred to the following options where a claim to privilege is disputed:

(a) finding that the evidence before the court does not establish the privilege, and ordering inspection;

(b) ordering further evidence to be produced on oath on the claim to privilege;

(c) inspecting the documents under CPR, r. 31.19 (for which see **48.23** and the principles laid down in *Atos Consulting Ltd v Avis Europe plc* [2007] EWHC 323 (TCC), [2008] Bus LR Digest D20); and

(d) ordering cross-examination of the witness making the claim to privilege under r. 32.7. This should be done only in an extreme case and where there is no alternative relief.

INSPECTION AND COPYING OF DOCUMENTS

48.21   There is in general no duty of confidence between opposing parties in litigation, so no restrictions (beyond the undertaking not to use documents for collateral purposes, see **48.33**, and any confidentiality undertakings a party is prepared to give) will be imposed as to which individuals will be allowed to inspect the documents on the inspecting party's side (*British Sky Broadcasting Group plc v Virgin Media Communications Ltd* [2008] EWCA Civ 612, *The Times*, 11 June 2008). Despite this, it seems that it is appropriate to require solicitors to give individual confidentiality undertakings where disclosed documents are commercially sensitive (*Interdigital Technology Corporation v Nokia Corporation* [2008] EWHC 969 (Pat), LTL 19/5/2008, where the undertakings were that the documents would remain at the solicitor's premises except to the extent necessary for making applications to the court and delivering papers to counsel, but no undertaking was required from counsel.

Inspection of documents referred to in statements of case, etc.

An appeal in *Expandable Ltd v Rubin* [2007] EWHC 2463 (Ch) was dismissed, see *Rubin v Expandable* **48.22** *Ltd* [2008] EWCA Civ 59, [2008] 1 WLR 1099. A document is 'mentioned' in another document within the meaning of CPR, r. 31.14(1), if it was specifically mentioned or directly alluded to. A comment in a witness statement that 'he wrote to me' was a direct allusion to the letter forming the basis of the comment. Upholding the decision at first instance, the fact that r. 31.14 applied to the letter did not waive any right or duty to object to inspection on the ground of privilege or public interest.

REFUSAL TO DISCLOSE OR PERMIT INSPECTION

Atos Consulting Ltd v Avis plc [2007] EWHC 323 (TCC) is reported as *Atos Consulting Ltd v Avis* **48.23** *Europe plc* [2007] EWHC 323 (TCC), [2008] Bus LR Digest D20. For the practice in anti-competition cases involving the Commission of the European Communities, see *Akzo Nobel Chemicals Ltd v Commission of the European Communities* (cases T-125 and T-253/03) [2008] Bus LR 348.

COLLATERAL USE OF DISCLOSED DOCUMENTS

There is a similar implied obligation on parties to an English arbitration not to disclose or use **48.33** documents prepared for and used in the arbitration for any purpose outside the arbitration (*Ali Shipping Corporation v Shipyard Trogir* [1999] 1 WLR 314).

Permission for collateral use

In relation to documents relating to an English arbitration, the High Court has jurisdiction to **48.35** grant restraining injunctions and declarations that the confidentiality obligation does not apply (*Michael Wilson and Partners Ltd v Emmott* [2008] EWCA Civ 184, [2008] Bus LR 1361). Generally, arbitration documents should be kept confidential, unless disclosure is required in the interests of justice (*Ali Shipping Corporation v Shipyard Trogir* [1999] 1 WLR 314), such as where a court might be misled if it does not have access to the documents (*Michael Wilson and Partners Ltd v Emmott*).

PRIVILEGE

Introduction

The burden of proof in a disputed claim for privilege rests on the person asserting the **48.37** privilege (*West London Pipeline and Storage Ltd v Total UK Ltd* [2008] EWHC 1729 (Comm), LTL 23/7/2008; *Akzo Nobel Chemicals Ltd v Commission of the European Communities* (cases T-125 and T-253/03) [2008] Bus LR 348).

PRIVILEGE AGAINST SELF-INCRIMINATION

Statutory limitations on the rule

Kensington International Ltd v Republic of Congo [2007] EWCA Civ 1128 is reported at [2008] 1 WLR **48.39** 1144.

LEGAL PROFESSIONAL PRIVILEGE

Legal advice privilege

48.44   **Legal advice**   Advice given by a solicitor who is known by the client to be struck-off is not protected by legal professional privilege (*Dadourian Group International Inc. v Simms* [2008] EWHC 1784 (Ch), LTL 1/8/2008).

48.46   **Examples of legal advice privilege**   A preparatory document drawn up by a client, even if created without the intention of sending it to the lawyer, may be protected by legal advice privilege, although such a claim has to be considered restrictively (*Akzo Nobel Chemicals Ltd v Commission of the European Communities* (cases T-125 and T-253/03) [2008] Bus LR 348). The mere fact a document has been discussed with a lawyer does not give it protection (*Akzo Nobel Chemicals Ltd v Commission of the European Communities*).

Iniquity

48.50   Add to point (b):

Where fraud between the solicitor and client is established in relation to the litigation itself, legal professional privilege is removed from all the relevant advice obtained in the litigation (*Dadourian Group International Inc. v Simms* [2008] EWHC; 1784 (Ch), LTL 1/8/2008).

WITHOUT-PREJUDICE COMMUNICATIONS

48.54   The *Chocoladefabriken Lindt & Sprungli AG v Nestlé Co. Ltd* [1978] RPC 287 principle (that a communication may be protected even where the words 'without prejudice' are not used) was applied in *Galliford Try Construction Ltd v Mott MacDonald Ltd* [2008] EWHC 603 (TCC), LTL 7/4/2008.

WAIVER OF PRIVILEGE

Implied waiver

48.60   Inclusion of a document in a list of documents (particularly where this was an obvious mistake) does not amount to a waiver of privilege (*Galliford Try Construction Ltd v Mott MacDonald Ltd* [2008] EWHC 603 (TCC), LTL 7/4/2008).

PRE-ACTION DISCLOSURE

Requirements for pre-action disclosure

48.71   Add to point (d):

In the case of a class of documents (see CPR, r. 31.16(3)(c)), the applicant must show that the whole class would be covered by standard disclosure (*Hutchison 3G UK Ltd v O2 (UK) Ltd* [2008] EWHC 55 (Comm), LTL 22/1/2008). There is no obligation on the respondent to specify which of the documents potentially within the class might be covered by standard disclosure (*Wakefield v Outhwaite* [1990] 2 Lloyd's Rep 157).

Add to point (e):

Pre-action disclosure of the medical records of a proposed claimant in a personal injuries claim was refused under r. 31.16(3)(d) in *OCS Group Ltd v Wells* [2008] EWHC 919 (QB), [2008] PIQR P18, where the court preferred the approach on medical records expressed in *Bennett v Compass Group UK and Ireland Ltd* [2002] EWCA Civ 642, [2002] ICR 1177, to that in *Black v*

Sumitomo Corporation [2001] EWCA Civ 1819, [2002] 1 WLR 1562. While medical records are relevant within the meaning of standard disclosure (rr. 31.6 and 31.16(3)(c)), as the issues between the parties will not have been precisely delineated at the time of most pre-action disclosure applications, such records may have little or no value in determining the claim, may increase the prospects of litigation, and may result in embarrassing information, unconnected to the claim, being disclosed to the defendant.

NORWICH PHARMACAL ORDERS

Under (d) add: **48.83**

The court will be very reluctant to order a bank to provide information under a *Norwich Pharmacal* order which involves a breach of confidence between a bank and its customer (*Koo Golden East Mongolia v Bank of Nova Scotia* [2007] EWCA Civ 1443, [2008] QB 717). In exercising its discretion the court will, where appropriate, take into account the principles in the Data Protection Act 1998 and the right to free speech in the ECHR, art. 10 (*Smith v ADVFN plc* [2008] EWHC 577 (QB), LTL 8/5/2008).

Add new point:

(e) The information sought is not protected by privilege, public interest, or state immunity. In *Koo Golden East Mongolia v Bank of Nova Scotia* [2007] EWCA Civ 1443, [2008] QB 717, the respondent was a central bank and was held entitled to claim State immunity under the State Immunity Act 1978, so relief was refused. In cases of possible privilege the court may alternatively grant the order, with the respondent taking the privilege point by way of objection to inspection under CPR, r 31.19.

Chapter 49   Witness Statements

STATEMENT OF TRUTH

For failing to sign a statement of truth, and making false statements to truth, see **23.13** and **49.9** **23.17** in this supplement.

Chapter 50   Affidavits

QUALIFICATION OF PERSON TAKING AN AFFIDAVIT

There is a £10 swearing fee, plus £2 per exhibit (CPFO, fee 12).   **50.3**

Chapter 52   Experts and Assessors

ADMISSIBILITY OF OPINION EVIDENCE

General rule

52.2 There are exceptions to the general rule that opinion evidence is inadmissible from lay witnesses in the case of inspectors' reports in winding-up proceedings (*Re St Piran Ltd* [1981] 1 WLR 1300) and evidence (from all sources) given by the Secretary of State in director disqualification proceedings (*Re Rex Williams Leisure Centre plc* [1994] Ch 350; *Secretary of State for Trade and Industry v Ashcroft* [1998] Ch 71; *Secretary of State for Business, Enterprise and Regulatory Reform v Aaron* (2008) LTL 5/6/2008).

WRITTEN REPORTS

Oral or written evidence at trial

52.26 The parties have a right to rely on the expert reports disclosed by other parties, unrestricted by any discretion in CPR, rr. 35.1 and 35.7, given the unqualified terms of r. 35.11 (*Shepherd Neame Ltd v EDF Energy Networks (SPN) plc* [2008] EWHC 123 (TCC), [2008] Bus LR Digest D43). The right to do so in r. 35.11 continues to apply after the instructing party drops out of the litigation. Even if there is a discretion to refuse permission to rely on a written report disclosed by an opposing party, there are strong countervailing factors in favour of granting permission, particularly where the relevant expert has taken part in joint discussions with other experts.

ASSESSORS

52.37 While it is appropriate to appoint assessors in technically complex or detailed cases, such as nautical collision claims, the Technology and Construction Court did not need the assistance of an assessor in a compulsory purchase quantum case involving consideration of the relevant government department's Compensation Code (*Balcombe Group plc v London Development Agency* [2008] EWHC 1392 (TCC), LTL 3/7/2008).

Chapter 53   Discontinuance

WHAT MAY BE DISCONTINUED

53.3 Arbitration claims under CPR, Part 62 (see **chapter 69**), are also subject to the rules on discontinuance in Part 38 (*Sheltam Rail Co. (Proprietary) Ltd v Mirambo Holdings Ltd* [2008] EWHC 829 (Comm), [2008] 2 Lloyd's Rep 195).

Chapter 54   Stays

STAYS TO PROTECT CONCURRENT CLAIMS

To point (a) add:

54.5

The court has an inherent jurisdiction to stay court proceedings which have been brought in breach of an agreement that any dispute should be resolved in a particular way, such as where there is an adjudication clause under the Housing Grants, Construction and Regeneration Act 1996 (*DGT Steel and Cladding Ltd v Cubitt Building and Interiors Ltd* [2007] EWHC 1587 (TCC), [2008] Bus LR 132). In *Ardentia Ltd v British Telecommunications plc* [2008] EWHC 2111 (Ch), LTL 23/6/2008, the contract between the parties contained a clause that they should refer disputes to alternative dispute resolution rather than litigation, except for applications for interim injunctions. This meant that the court could only deal with interim injunction applications: making such an application did not open the door to the court having jurisdiction over the substantive dispute.

To point (d) add:

The court may grant a stay to ensure that related proceedings in different jurisdictions are tried in a particular order if there are very strong grounds for doing so for case management reasons (*Reichhold Norway ASA v Goldman Sachs International* [2000] 1 WLR 173). The risk of irreconcilable judgments may be sufficient for this purpose (*Curtis v Lockheed Martin UK Holdings Ltd* [2008] EWHC 260 (Comm), [2008] 1 CLC 219, where the application was refused).

Chapter 56   Giving Evidence without Attending Court

EXAMINATION OUT OF THE JURISDICTION

Requests to EU Regulation States

Regulation (EC) No. 1206/2001 does not apply to applications for disclosure of assets orders against non-parties ancillary to freezing injunctions (see **38.25**). This is because there is no request for the taking of evidence in another member State (*Masri v Consolidated Contractors International Co. SAL* [2008] EWCA Civ 876, LTL 28/7/2008).

56.8

INJUNCTION TO RESTRAIN THREATS TO WITNESS OUTSIDE JURISDICTION

In *Masood v Zahoor* [2008] EWHC 328 (Ch), LTL 4/4/2008, an injunction was granted restraining the defendant for the duration of the proceedings from threatening a witness with disciplinary proceedings or taking any step in the witness' country which might inhibit or prohibit the witness from giving evidence in the English proceedings.

56.16

Chapter 59   Trial

PRE-TRIAL CHECKLISTS AND FIXING THE DATE FOR TRIAL

Multi-track listing

59.4   Very cogent reasons are required before the court will accede to an application to bring forward a trial date, given the effect on other litigants in the queue of cases waiting to be heard (*W. L. Gore and Associates GmbH v Geox SpA* [2008] EWHC 462 (Pat), LTL 7/4/2008).

ADJOURNMENT

Problems obtaining representation

59.10   The availability of counsel of choice, particularly where replacement counsel will have to spend a substantial amount of time reading into the case, or where the client reposes a great deal of confidence in existing counsel, are factors to be taken into account in deciding whether to grant an adjournment (*Collins v Gordon* [2008] EWCA Civ 110, LTL 21/1/2008). Where the problem is self-induced, such as through dismissing solicitors shortly before the hearing, a short adjournment may be all that the court should grant (*Property Investor's Courses Ltd v Secretary of State for Trade and Industry* [2008] EWCA Civ 872, LTL 14/7/2008, where the court granted a two-day adjournment in a straightforward case).

Breach of case management directions

59.11   PD 28, para. 5.4, and PD 29, para. 7.4, only apply where there has been a breach of case management directions, and not where an adjournment is sought on the basis of unavailability of counsel or witnesses (*Collins v Gordon* [2008] EWCA Civ 110, LTL 21/1/2008).

In *Gilbart v Thomas Graham* [2008] EWCA Civ 897, LTL 24/6/2008, the Court of Appeal overturned a decision to refuse an adjournment of the trial date in order to give effect to the overriding objective. The application had been made 21 days before the date for the trial, which was an unrealistically short time for the defendant (who had applied for the adjournment) to obtain specific disclosure from the claimant and to instruct an expert on a loss of profits claim. In *Ratiopharm (UK) Ltd v Alza Corporation* [2008] EWHC 1182 (Ch), LTL 1/5/2008, six months was regarded as enough time to prepare a patent infringement claim for trial (the party seeking to avoid the trial date having received a letter with the allegations in the litigation 13 months before the trial date).

PRE-TRIAL ARRANGEMENTS

Rights of audience

59.30   Practice Direction (Court Dress) (No. 4) [2008] 1 WLR 357 has been made to ensure that solicitors and other advocates authorised under the Courts and Legal Services Act 1990 are no longer precluded from wearing wigs when appearing in court. It revokes Practice Direction (Court Dress) [1994] 1 WLR 1056; Practice Direction (Court Dress) (No. 2) [1995] 1 WLR 648 and Practice Direction (Court Dress) (No. 3) [1998] 1 WLR 1764.

Dress requirements for advocates appearing in the Supreme Court and in county courts are:

- Queen's Counsel wear a short wig and a silk (or stuff) gown over a court coat;
- junior counsel wear a short wig and stuff gown with bands;
- solicitors and other advocates authorised under the Courts and Legal Services Act 1990

wear a black solicitor's gown with bands, and they may wear short wigs in circumstances where they would be worn by Queen's Counsel or junior counsel.

Members of the Association of Law Costs Draftsmen may be certified by the Association with rights of audience (Association of Law Costs Draftsmen Order 2006 (SI 2006/3333)).

CONDUCT OF THE TRIAL

Deciding between witnesses

Cases are decided by the quality of the evidence adduced at the trial, not by weight of numbers of witnesses on one side compared to the other (*Gurney Consulting Engineers v Gleeds Health and Safety Ltd* [2006] EWHC 43 (TCC) at [11]). **59.48**

Adjudicating on expert evidence

The trial judge is entitled to rely on additional or revised evidence on an unresolved issue from an expert based on further experiments conducted by the expert after a pre-trial meeting of the experts and before or during the hearing (*Aintree Hospitals NHS Trust v Sutcliffe* [2008] EWCA Civ 179, [2008] LS Law Med 230). **59.49**

Chapter 60   Non-attendance

NON-ATTENDANCE AT TRIAL

An appeal court may treat an appeal as an application to set aside for non-attendance, applying the principles set out in CPR, r. 39.3 (*Zambia v Meer Care and Desai* [2008] EWCA Civ 754, LTL 9/7/2008). There may be 'good reason' for non-attendance within the meaning of r. 39.3(5) where there was no letter of claim, several of the court documents were not translated into the defendant's language, and the defendant thought the documents required his involvement as a witness rather than as a party (*Zambia v Meer Care and Desai*). **60.2**

The fact there is a pleaded defence does not mean it has a reasonable prospect of success (*Sinclair v Johnson* [2008] EWCA Civ 667, LTL 23/5/2008).

Chapter 61   Judgments and Orders

FORM OF JUDGMENTS AND ORDERS

Consent orders

There is a long-established distinction between a true consent order, which has contractual effect and cannot be appealed, and a situation where an order is marked 'by consent', but in reality is one where one side did no more than not object to the order being made (*Siebe Gorman and Co. Ltd v Pneupac Ltd* [1982] 1 WLR 185; *Martin v Triggs Turner Barton* [2008] EWHC 89 (Ch), *The Times*, 5 February 2008). **61.11**

In *Chanel Ltd v F. W. Woolworth and Co. Ltd* [1981] 1 WLR 485 a respondent was not permitted to reopen an interim order, previously disposed of by consent, on the ground that a subsequent authority had undermined the applicant's case. In *Di Placito v Slater* [2003] EWCA Civ 1863,

[2004] 1 WLR 1605, the court refused permission to an applicant to be relieved from an undertaking previously given by consent. These cases were distinguished in *Kensington International Ltd v Republic of Congo* [2007] EWCA Civ 1128, [2008] 1 WLR 1144, where there was a clear difference between the matter previously disposed of by consent and the present application. The consent order had conceded that the respondent was under no obligation to disclose information about cargoes on a continuing basis from a stated date. The current application was for disclosure relating to two specific voyages, which was regarded as a different order made in different circumstances from the consent order.

Interim payments

61.19 PD 40B, paras 5.1 and 5.1A (as amended by the 47th Update with effect from 1 October 2008), add further detail to the form of interim payment orders where there are recoverable benefits or lump-sum awards affected by the Social Security (Recovery of Benefits) Act 1997. See also **36.15** in this supplement.

Periodical payments

61.26 In deciding whether to make a periodical payments order, and in what form, the court's overall aim is to make whatever order objectively best meets the claimant's needs (*Tameside and Glossop Acute Services NHS Trust v Thompstone* [2008] EWCA Civ 5, [2008] 2 All ER 553). The court performs an inquisitorial role in doing this, in which there are no legal burdens of proof.

The Damages Act 1996, s. 2(8), provides that an order for periodical payments is to be treated as providing for the amount of the payments to vary by reference to the retail prices index at such times and in such manner as might be determined or in accordance with the CPR. This may be disapplied or modified by the court under s. 2(9). There are no restrictions on the types of modifications that may be made under s. 2(9)(b)), which may include substituting a measure based on annual earnings and converted into an index in place of the retail prices index (*Tameside and Glossop Acute Services NHS Trust v Thompstone* at [4] to [43]). In deciding on a suitable index (see [52] to [58]), the court considers:

(a) the accuracy of the match of the particular data series to the loss and expenditure being compensated;
(b) the authority of the collector of the data;
(c) statistical reliability;
(d) accessibility;
(e) consistency over time;
(f) reproducibility in the future; and
(g) simplicity and consistency in application.

In considering the defendant's preferences under PD 41B, para. 1, usually it is sufficient if these are placed before the court on instructions, without the need to call expert evidence. There is no bar on a defendant adducing the evidence of a financial advice expert (to oppose that of the claimant), but it would be rare for permission to be granted (*Tameside and Glossop Acute Services NHS Trust v Thompstone* at [109] to [112]).

EMBARGOED JUDGMENTS

61.30 *Egan v Motor Services (Bath) Ltd* [2007] EWCA Civ 1002 is reported at [2008] 1 WLR 1589. In *R (Edwards) v Environment Agency* [2008] UKHL 22, [2008] 1 WLR 1587, Lord Hoffmann said, at [66], that sending a 27-paragraph memorandum of submissions commenting on draft speeches was an abuse of process. The purpose of disclosing draft speeches is to obtain the help of counsel in correcting inadvertent errors and ambiguities. It is not to enable counsel to reargue the case. *Crown Prosecution Service v P* [2007] EWHC 1131 (Admin) is now reported as *Director of Public Prosecutions v P (No. 2)* [2007] EWHC 1144 (Admin), [2008] 1 WLR 1024. If a solicitor is in doubt as to the propriety of a particular disclosure, a request should be made by email to the judge's clerk for permission (see *Director of Public Prosecutions v P (No. 2)* at [15]).

In the light of these decisions, PD 40E has been reissued (with effect from 1 October 2008). It applies to reserved judgments in all courts (para. 1.1). The new PD 40E adopts the main provisions on the availability of reserved judgments before handing down and correction to the draft judgment, from the old PD 40E (new paras 2.1 to 2.4, 2.8, 2.9 and 3.1). New provisions are:

Availability of Reserved Judgments before Handing Down

2.5 Where a copy of the draft judgment is supplied to a party's legal representatives in electronic form, they may supply a copy to that party in the same form.

2.6 If a party to whom a copy of the draft judgment is supplied under para. 2.4 is a partnership, company, government department, local authority or other organisation of a similar nature, additional copies may be distributed in confidence within the organisation, provided that all reasonable steps are taken to preserve its confidential nature and the requirements of para. 2.4 are adhered to.

2.7 If the parties or their legal representatives are in any doubt about the persons to whom copies of the draft judgment may be distributed they should enquire of the judge or presiding judge.

Orders Consequential on Judgment

4.1 Following the circulation of the draft judgment the parties or their legal representatives must seek to agree orders consequential upon the judgment.

4.2 In respect of any draft agreed order the parties must:

(a) fax or email a copy to the clerk to the judge or presiding judge (together with any proposed corrections or amendments to the draft judgment); and
(b) file four copies (with completed backsheets) in the relevant court office, by 12 noon on the working day before handing down.

4.3 A copy of a draft order must bear the case reference, the date of handing down and the name of the judge or presiding judge.

4.4 Where a party wishes to apply for an order consequential on the judgment the application must be made by filing written submissions with the clerk to the judge or presiding judge by 12 noon on the working day before handing down.

4.5 Unless the court orders otherwise:

(a) where judgment is to be given by an appeal court (which has the same meaning as in r. 52.1(3)(b)), the application will be determined without a hearing; and
(b) where judgment is to be given by any other court, the application will be determined at a hearing.

Attendance at Handing Down

5.1 If there is not to be an oral hearing of an application for an order consequential on judgment:

(a) the parties' advocates need not attend on the handing down of judgment; and
(b) the judgment may be handed down by a judge sitting alone.

5.2 Where para. 5.1(a) applies but an advocate does attend the handing down of judgment, the court may if it considers such attendance unnecessary, disallow the costs of the attendance.

REVIEW OF JUDGMENT

Reconsideration of case management decisions

61.39 A change in a party's appreciation of the effect of an order is simply a change in perception, not a change of circumstances, and does not justify reconsideration of the earlier decision (*W. L. Gore and Associates GmbH v Geox SpA* [2008] EWHC 462 (Pat), LTL 7/4/2008).

Chapter 62   Interest

RATE OF INTEREST

Commercial claims

62.22 A rate of 2 per cent above base rate was applied in *Adinstone Ltd v Gatt* (2008) LTL 18/6/2008, being the rate established by the evidence as the rate on the claimant's overdraft facility, and the rate anyone dealing with the claimant might have expected it to pay (applying *Jaura v Ahmed* [2002] EWCA Civ 210, *The Times*, 18 March 2002).

INTEREST ON JUDGMENT DEBTS

62.29 An arbitration award registered as a judgment under the Arbitration Act 1996, s. 100, attracts interest at the usual Judgments Act 1838, s. 17, rate of 8 per cent per annum, subject to the court's discretion to disallow interest under CPR, r. 40.8(1)(b) (*Gater Assets Ltd v NAK Naftogaz Ukrainiy* [2008] EWHC 1108 (Comm), LTL 28/5/2008).

INTEREST ON COSTS

62.30 The conventional rate of interest on costs until the date of assessment before the costs judge is 1 per cent above base rate (*National Westminster Bank plc v Rabobank Nederland (No. 2)* [2007] EWHC 1742 (Comm), [2008] 1 All ER (Comm) 243). It is for the paying party to introduce evidence that some other rate should be applied. Expert evidence will be required if it is asserted that a body with the financial substance of the receiving party could borrow money below this rate. Second-hand expressions of understanding are not a safe basis for departing from the conventional rate (*National Westminster Bank plc v Rabobank Nederland (No. 2)*).

A rate of 1 per cent above base rate was applied to an order for the repayment of an interim payment in respect of costs in *Multiplex Construction Ltd v Cleveland Bridge Ltd* [2008] EWCA Civ 133, LTL 9/4/2008. The power to award interest in this situation derives from CPR, rr. 44.3(6)(g) and 44.3(8).

Chapter 63   Solicitor and Own Client Costs

AGREEING SOLICITORS' CHARGES

Mastercigars Direct Ltd v Withers LLP [2007] EWHC 2733 (Ch) is reported at [2008] 3 All ER 417.   **63.2**

The point made in the text about the importance of identifying who is responsible for the solicitor's charges is illustrated by *Lygoe v Ilsley* [2008] EWHC 831 (QB), LTL 28/4/2008, where the court found the solicitor's case that an individual was personally liable for its fees for work done for various companies was implausible in the absence of an agreement in writing.

CLIENT CARE

Client care letter and client estimates

It is advisable, but not an absolute requirement, that a solicitor acting for a client who may   **63.6** join in group litigation should say in the client care letter that some of the work done would be for the benefit of the group, and the individual client will be liable only for his share (*Brown v Russell Young and Co.* [2007] EWCA Civ 43, [2008] 1 WLR 525). Where different parties represented in group litigation have different solicitors, the agreements between the solicitors should clearly define the arrangements for sharing the costs of generic work for the group. It is also sensible for careful records to be kept of the number of clients each solicitor is acting for at any specific time.

ESTIMATES

The solicitor was held bound by its estimate in *Reynolds v Stone Rowe Brewer* [2008] EWHC 497   **63.19** (QB), LTL 1/4/2008.

Chapter 64   Part 36 Offers

NON-DISCLOSURE

Non-disclosure of Part 36 offers

The restriction on disclosure of Part 36 offers in CPR, r. 36.13(2), applies to the trial judge,   **64.4** so does not prevent the offer being referred to the judge dealing with an application for summary judgment or striking out on the question of costs arising from that application, even if remedies have yet to be decided (*Experience Hendrix v Times Newspapers Ltd* [2008] EWHC 458 (Ch), LTL 14/3/2008). If this happens, other without-prejudice correspondence may be referred to in order to ensure the judge is not given a distorted picture (*Experience Hendrix v Times Newspapers Ltd*).

OFFERS TO SETTLE UNDER THE NEW CPR, PART 36

Personal injury claims: deduction of benefits

CPR, r. 36.15, is amended with effect from 1 October 2008 by the Civil Procedure   **64.11** (Amendment) Rules 2008 (SI 2008/2178). The amendment expands the deduction of benefits provisions, which formerly applied to recoverable benefits under the Social Security (Recovery of Benefits) Act 1997, to lump-sum payments under the Social Security (Recovery of Benefits) (Lump Sum Payments) Regulations 2008 (SI 2008/1596). The main provisions of r. 36.15 (particularly paras (3) to (6)) remain unchanged, and require Part 36 payments to include statements of the gross compensation, the name and amount of any deductible benefits, and the net amount after deduction of benefits. 'Recoverable lump sum payments' has the same meaning as in the Social Security (Recovery of Benefits) (Lump Sum Payments) Regulations 2008, reg. 4, and 'deductible amount' now includes any lump sum payment by the amount of which damages are to be reduced in accordance with reg. 12 ('deductible lump sum payments') (CPR, r. 36.15(1)).

COSTS CONSEQUENCES OF NON-ACCEPTANCE

Failing to obtain a judgment more advantageous than a Part 36 offer

64.36 In *Carver v BAA plc* [2008] EWCA Civ 412, [2008] 3 All ER 911, it was held that the post-6 April 2007 version of CPR, Part 36, has fundamentally changed the concept of beating an offer to settle. The phrase used in r. 36.14(1)(a) is whether the claimant fails to obtain a judgment which is 'more advantageous' than the defendant's Part 36 offer. In *Hall v Stone* [2007] EWCA Civ 1354, *The Times*, 1 February 2008, Smith LJ said, at [82]: 'In these days where both sides are expected to conduct themselves in a reasonable way and to seek agreement where possible, it may be right to penalise a party to some degree for failing to accept a reasonable offer or for failing to come back with a counter-offer'.

In *Carver v BAA plc* Ward LJ said, at [30] and [31], that the phrase 'more advantageous' is more open-textured than the former phrase 'fails to better' in the pre-2007 version of Part 36. It permits a more wide-ranging review of the circumstances of the case, including taking a view on whether the eventual judgment was 'worth the fight'. The court can therefore consider matters such as the costs incurred after the offer, and the emotional stress of taking the case to trial. On the facts, costs were about £80,000, and the judgment in the sum of £4,686 was effectively only £51 more than the Part 36 offer. While the claimant was awarded her costs up to the end of the relevant period (see **64.16**), there was no order as to costs thereafter.

In a defamation claim, comparing the terms of an offer with the eventual judgment may, depending on the terms of the offer and the events at trial, involve considering the terms and value of any apology and any damage to the reputation of the claimant arising from the evidence given at the trial (*Jones v Associated Newspapers Ltd* [2007] EWHC 1489 (QB), [2008] 1 All ER 240).

Chapter 65   Security for Costs

THE RESPONDENT

Claimants

65.3 *Gater Assets Ltd v NAK Naftogaz Ukrainiy* [2007] EWCA Civ 988 is reported at [2008] Bus LR 388.

CONDITIONS FOR ORDERING SECURITY FOR COSTS

Impecunious limited company

65.12 The jurisdiction to order security for costs against companies under CPR, r. 25.13(2)(c), is available against unlimited companies, and also companies with a single member (*Jirehouse Capital v Beller* [2008] EWCA Civ 908, [2008] BCC 636). The question whether there is 'reason to believe' the company would not be able to pay an order for costs is one of evaluating the risk, and does not have to be established on the balance of probabilities. No gloss (such as the phrase 'in significant danger' used in *Re Unisoft Group Ltd (No. 2)* [1993] BCLC 532) should be put on the words of the test in the rule (*Jirehouse Capital v Beller*). A company in liquidation will meet the test (*Hart Investments Ltd v Larchpark Ltd* [2007] EWHC 291 (TCC), [2008] 1 BCLC 589).

AMOUNT

65.25 The amount ordered should be neither illusory nor oppressive (*Hart Investments Ltd v Larchpark Ltd* [2007] EWHC 291 (TCC), [2008] 1 BCLC 589). While security for costs can include pre-action costs, the court should be slow to exercise its discretion to include these as there is a risk that such an order could become penal in nature (*Lobster Group Ltd v Heidelberg Graphic Equipment Ltd* [2008] EWHC 413 (TCC), [2008] 2 All ER 1173).

ORDER

65.26 After-the-event insurance is unlikely to provide a satisfactory alternative to the usual payments in or bank guarantees by way of security for costs (*Belco Trading Co. v Kondo* [2008] EWCA Civ 205, LTL 4/6/2008).

Chapter 66   Costs Orders

GENERAL PRINCIPLES

Partial success

66.11 **Partial success to be taken into account**   In general, a claimant who succeeds on primary liability is regarded as the overall winner, despite a finding of contributory negligence (*'Krysia' Maritime Inc. v Intership Ltd* [2008] EWHC 1880 (Admlty), LTL 12/8/2008, where it was also held the principle is the same in the Admiralty Court). There may be exceptions where the primary issue is the degree of contributory negligence, or where there is a finding of very substantial contributory negligence.

A successful party may be deprived of some of its costs where the issue or issues on which it was unsuccessful are discrete, and where the case is sufficiently exceptional to justify depriving the winner of some of its costs (*SmithKline Beecham plc v Apotex Europe Ltd (No. 2)* [2004] EWCA Civ 1703, [2005] 2 Costs LR 293; *Qualcomm Inc. v Nokia Corporation* [2008] EWHC 777 (Ch), LTL 20/5/2008).

66.13 **Percentage or issues-based costs orders**   It may be appropriate to make an issues-based costs order (rather than a percentage order) where there is a substantial imbalance between the amount of costs incurred by the different parties (*Research in Motion UK Ltd v Visto Corporation* [2008] EWHC 819 (Pat), LTL 22/4/2008). Such orders are unusual, though, because it is highly undesirable to make a costs order which results in the assessment of both sides' costs, and the disparity has to be substantial before this can be justified (*Abbott Laboratories Ltd v Evysio Medical Devices ULC* [2008] EWHC 1083 (Pat), LTL 21/5/2008).

There is a well-established 'double deduction' rule when making a percentage costs order (e.g., *Earl of Malmesbury v Strutt and Parker* [2008] EWHC 424 (QB), LTL 31/3/2008). Under this, if the claimant wins, but the defendant is successful on an issue representing 7.5 per cent of the claimant's costs, the claimant would be awarded 85 per cent of its costs (the 15 per cent deduction covering the 7.5 per cent of the claimant's costs on the issue he lost, and 7.5 per cent of the defendant's costs, representing the proportion attributable to that issue which the claimant ought to pay). This rule is not applied mechanically. It is not a matter of simply calculating how many hours of the trial were taken up with the lost issue compared with the whole trial, or counting pages of the trial transcript (*Abbott Laboratories Ltd v Evysio Medical Devices ULC*). Often the judge needs to take into account work done before trial, the relative expense of the evidence required on the different issues, and the degree of overlap in investigating the successful and unsuccessful issues.

Misconduct by the successful party

66.19 **Refusal to participate in ADR**   Where a failure to mediate was caused by unreasonable attitudes taken by both sides, it is not open to the losing party to use the winner's failure as a basis for an adverse costs order (*Earl of Malmesbury v Strutt and Parker* [2008] EWHC 424 (QB), LTL 31/3/2008). A party who agrees to mediation and takes an unreasonable stance in the mediation is in the same position as a party who unreasonably refuses to mediate at all (*Earl of Malmesbury v Strutt and Parker*).

The problems in identifying the best time to attempt to resolve a dispute through ADR were recognised by HHJ Peter Coulson QC in *Nigel Witham Ltd v Smith* [2008] EWHC 12 (TCC), [2008] CILL 2557. Premature references can waste costs, and delay can mean the case passes the point where costs already expended make settlement almost impossible.

Indemnity-basis costs to reflect misconduct

66.21 Point (c). Where the application is for indemnity-basis costs of the proceedings, it is necessary to consider the criticised conduct in the context of the entire litigation. It is not the character of the misconduct which engages the court's discretion, but the justice of the circumstances in which the receiving party became involved in the proceedings. There is an important difference between mere errors of judgment in the conduct of a case and behaviour resulting in the overall unreasonable or unsatisfactory conduct of the litigation (*National Westminster Bank plc v Rabobank Nederland (No. 2)* [2007] EWHC 1742 (Comm), [2008] 1 All ER (Comm) 243).

Point (f). Other first-instance cases making indemnity-basis costs orders for breach of jurisdiction, anti-suit and arbitration clauses are *Kyrgyz Mobil Tel Ltd v Fellowes International Holdings Ltd* [2005] EWHC 1314 (Comm) and *National Westminster Bank plc v Rabobank Nederland (No. 3)* [2007] EWHC 1742 (Comm), [2008] 1 All ER (Comm) 266. A similar approach was adopted when a party took an unmeritorious point over jurisdiction in an adjudication case (*Harris Calnan Construction Co. Ltd v Ridgewood (Kensington) Ltd* [2007] EWHC 2738 (TCC), [2008] Bus LR 636). In *C v D* [2007] EWCA Civ 1282, [2008] Bus LR 843, Longmore LJ declined to come to a definitive conclusion on the proper approach on this question (at [32]), and made a standard-basis costs order on the facts of the case (which was based on the doctrine that agreement on the seat of an arbitration was analogous to an exclusive jurisdiction clause, as opposed to being an actual jurisdiction clause).

In some cases the claimant will be able to formulate a claim for an anti-suit injunction as a separate claim for breach of a jurisdiction clause or anti-suit clause. In these cases the successful party may have a claim for damages representing the costs of defending any proceedings brought in breach of the clause, and may also be entitled to the costs of the

English proceedings for the injunction. The claim for costs as damages is assessed on the indemnity basis (*National Westminster Bank plc v Rabobank Nederland (No. 3)* [2007] EWHC 1742 (Comm), [2008] 1 All ER (Comm) 266).

INTERIM COSTS ORDERS

It is usual to reserve costs in applications for interim injunctions (*Picnic at Ascot Inc. v Derigs*   **66.26**
[2001] FSR 2). This is not an invariable rule (*Albon v Naza Motor Trading Sdn Bhd (No. 4)* [2007] EWCA Civ 1124, [2008] 1 All ER (Comm) 351, at [21]), particularly where the interim injunction is granted on an issue which is unlikely to be determined at trial. It is usual to order costs of the proceedings in favour of a successful applicant in a summary judgement or striking out application, even if remedies are left over to be determined later (*Experience Hendrix v Times Newspapers Ltd* [2008] EWHC 458 (Ch), LTL 14/3/2008).

MULTIPLE PARTIES AND CLAIMS

Counterclaims

The principles in *Medway Oil and Storage Co. Ltd v Continental Contractors Ltd* [1929] AC 88 were   **66.44**
regarded as technical in *Bateman v Joyce* (2008) LTL 26/6/2008 (SCCO), so that a consent order would ordinarily be taken as adopting those principles only if words such as 'for the avoidance of doubt the principle in *Medway Oil* applies' were used.

BEDDOE ORDERS

Protective costs orders

Procedure for seeking a PCO, point (c), add: **66.52**

If the order is granted, the defendant has the right to apply to have the order set aside, but has to show compelling reasons to alter the order (*R (Compton) v Wiltshire Primary Care Trust* [2008] EWCA Civ 749, LTL 1/7/2008).

The same procedure applies to appeals to the Court of Appeal (*R (Compton) v Wiltshire Primary Care Trust*).

Principles laid down in *R (Corner House Research) v Secretary of State for Trade and Industry* [2005] EWCA Civ 192, [2005] 1 WLR 2600, add to point (a):

An issue may be of 'general public importance' if it affects a wide community, such as the closure of a unit at an NHS hospital. There is no requirement that the issue has to be of interest to all the public nationally (*R (Compton) v Wiltshire Primary Care Trust*).

GROUP LITIGATION

Generic costs incurred in what was intended to be group litigation, but which was settled   **66.55**
before proceedings were issued (and hence before a GLO was made) are recoverable in a detailed assessment following a Part 8 application under CPR, r. 44.12A (*Brown v Russell Young and Co.* [2007] EWCA Civ 43, [2008] 1 WLR 525).

NON-PARTY COSTS ORDERS

66.66 A non-party costs order can be made against a receiver of a company, particularly where the receiver is the 'real' party. A costs order is more readily available against a receiver where the company has gone into liquidation, or where the successful party has not been able to obtain security for costs or adequate security for costs (*Mills v Birchall* [2008] EWCA Civ 385, [2008] BCC 471). An order will not be made unless the non-party funding has caused the applicant to incur costs he would not otherwise have incurred (*Jackson v Thakrar* [2007] EWHC 626 (TCC), [2008] 1 All ER 601). It will be exceptional to make a non-party costs order where the applicant had a cause of action against the non-party and did not join them to the proceedings (*Oriakhel v Vickers* [2008] EWCA Civ 748, LTL 4/7/2008).

Non-party costs orders were made against liability insurers which had funded, controlled and directed litigation involving their insurance clients for their own benefit in *Plymouth and South West Co-operative Society Ltd v Architecture, Structure and Management Ltd* [2006] EWHC 3252 (TCC), [2007] Lloyd's Rep I and R 596 and *Palmer v Palmer* [2008] EWCA Civ 46, LTL 6/2/2008.

WASTED COSTS ORDERS

66.70 There will be no causation where the costs sought were incurred before the alleged default (*Hedrich v Standard Bank London Ltd* [2008] EWCA Civ 905, LTL 30/7/2008), or if they would have been incurred anyway.

Wasted costs applications follow a fair, simple and summary procedure which should take hours rather than days (*Ridehalgh v Horsefield* [1994] Ch 205, and see **66.71**). If investigation of the issues on a wasted costs application cannot be achieved within these parameters, the application should be refused (*Hedrich v Standard Bank London Ltd*).

Examples of wasted costs

66.72 Defective, and even confused, disclosure is not the same thing as the lawyer being in breach of his duty to the court, and did not merit a wasted costs order (*Hedrich v Standard Bank London Ltd*).

Chapter 67   Fixed and Predictable Costs on Judgments etc.

SITUATIONS WHERE FIXED COSTS APPLY

67.3 As expressly stated in CPR, r. 45.1(1), the court has a discretion to award full costs in cases where otherwise fixed costs will apply, see *Amber Construction Services Ltd v London Interspace HG Ltd* [2007] EWHC 3042 (TCC), [2008] BLR 74.

PREDICTABLE COSTS IN ROAD TRAFFIC ACCIDENT CLAIMS

Disputes covered by the scheme

67.8 Where a claim arises from a road traffic accident, such as where a passenger is injured when alighting from a coach, the predictable costs scheme in CPR, rr. 45.7 to 45.14, applies and is not displaced by pleading the claim under the Occupiers' Liability Act 1957 or on any other legal basis (*Green v Kis Coaches and Taxis Ltd* (2008) LTL 13/5/2008 (Plymouth County Court)).

Amount recoverable

The 12.5 per cent success fee recoverable under CPR, r. 45.11(1), is a matter of entitlement, **67.9**
not discretion (*Kilby v Gawith* [2008] EWCA Civ 812, *The Times*, 13 June 2008, applying *Lamont v Burton* [2007] EWCA Civ 429, [2007] 1 WLR 2814; see **67.17**).

Chapter 68   Assessment of Costs

INTERIM PAYMENT ON ACCOUNT OF COSTS

A stay on payment of an interim payment on account of costs may be ordered where **68.8**
immediate payment runs the risk that justice will not be done, for example, where there is
an appeal (*Renewable Power and Light plc v Renewable Power and Light Services Inc.* (2008) LTL
7/4/2008).

DETAILED ASSESSMENT

Bill of costs

Where the receiving party was represented by different solicitors during the course of **68.12**
proceedings, the bill should be divided into different parts so as to distinguish between the
costs payable in respect of each solicitor (PD 43–48, para. 4.2(2)). If the receiving party fails
to do this, and the costs judge completes the assessment and issues a final certificate, the
receiving party cannot claim a further assessment of the omitted costs (*Moat Housing Group-
South Ltd v Harris (No. 2)* [2007] EWHC 3092 (QB), [2008] 1 WLR 1578). If one of the firms' costs
are omitted from the bill, and the parties agree the costs in the bill, whether the bill can be
amended depends on the construction of the agreement, and whether the receiving party
has communicated an intention to make a later claim for the costs incurred by the other
solicitors.

Assessment hearing

Members of the Association of Law Costs Draftsmen may be certified by the Association with **68.17**
rights of audience (Association of Law Costs Draftsmen Order 2006 (SI 2006/3333)).

INDEMNITY PRINCIPLE

A new exception to the indemnity principle is created by the Legal Services Act 2007, s. 194, **68.28**
which provides:

194. Payments in respect of pro bono representation

(1) This section applies to proceedings in a civil court in which—
   (a) a party to the proceedings ('P') is or was represented by a legal representative ('R'),
       and
   (b) R's representation of P is or was provided free of charge, in whole or in part.
(2) This section applies to such proceedings even if P is or was also represented by a legal
    representative not acting free of charge.
(3) The court may order any person to make a payment to the prescribed charity in respect of
    R's representation of P (or, if only part of R's representation of P was provided free of
    charge, in respect of that part).

(4) In considering whether to make such an order and the terms of such an order, the court must have regard to—

    (a) whether, had R's representation of P not been provided free of charge, it would have ordered the person to make a payment to P in respect of the costs payable to R by P in respect of that representation, and

    (b) if it would, what the terms of the order would have been.

(5) The court may not make an order under subsection (3) against a person represented in the proceedings if the person's representation was at all times within subsection (6).

(6) Representation is within this subsection if it is—

    (a) provided by a legal representative acting free of charge, or

    (b) funded by the Legal Services Commission as part of the Community Legal Service.

(7) Rules of court may make further provision as to the making of orders under subsection (3), and may in particular—

    (a) provide that such orders may not be made in civil proceedings of a description specified in the rules;

    (b) make provision about the procedure to be followed in relation to such orders;

    (c) specify matters (in addition to those mentioned in subsection (4)) to which the court must have regard in deciding whether to make such an order, and the terms of any order.

(8) 'The prescribed charity' means the charity prescribed by order made by the Lord Chancellor.

(9) An order under subsection (8) may only prescribe a charity which—

    (a) is registered in accordance with section 3A of the Charities Act 1993 (c. 10), and

    (b) provides financial support to persons who provide, or organise or facilitate the provision of, legal advice or assistance (by way of representation or otherwise) which is free of charge.

(10) In this section—

'legal representative', in relation to a party to proceedings, means a person exercising a right of audience or conducting litigation on the party's behalf;

'civil court' means the civil division of the Court of Appeal, the High Court, or any county court;

'free of charge' means otherwise than for or in expectation of fee, gain or reward.

(11) The court may not make an order under subsection (3) in respect of representation if (or to the extent that) it is provided before this section comes into force.

With effect from 1 October 2008, the Civil Procedure (Amendment) Rules 2008, SI 2008/2178) introduces CPR, r. 44.3C, dealing with orders under s. 194(3). This provides, by r. 44.3C(2)(a), that such an order will be for fixed costs under Part 45 where Part 45 would otherwise apply. Where Part 45 does not apply, by r. 44.3C(2)(b), the court may determine the amount of the payment (other than a sum equivalent to fixed costs) to be made by the paying party to the prescribed charity by:

(a) making a summary assessment; or

(b) making an order for detailed assessment,

    of a sum equivalent to all or part of the costs the paying party would have been ordered to pay to the party with pro bono representation in respect of that representation had it not been provided free of charge.

Under PD 43–48, paras 10A.1 and 13.2, the general rule is that the court will make a summary assessment of costs in the circumstances unless there is good reason not to do so. To assist the court in making a summary assessment of the amount payable to the prescribed charity, the party who has pro bono representation must prepare, file and serve, in accordance with para. 13.5(2), a written statement of the sum equivalent to the costs that party would have claimed for that legal representation had it not been provided free of charge (para. 10A.2).

Where there is an order for detailed assessment and the receiving party had pro bono representation for part only of the proceedings, the bill of costs must be divided into different parts to differentiate between the different periods of funding (PD 43–48, para. 4.2(1A)). The bill of costs must not include a claim for VAT in respect of the pro bono costs (para. 5.21).

An order under the Legal Services Act 2007, s. 194(3), must specify that the payment by the paying party must be made to the prescribed charity (CPR, r. 44.3C(3)). The receiving party is required to keep the prescribed charity informed by sending it copies of relevant orders and certificates (r. 44.3C(4), order under s. 194(3): r. 47.5(4), default costs certificate; r. 47.12(5), order setting aside or varying default costs certificate; r. 47.16(6), final costs certificate).

Disclosure of documents to paying party

See *Gower Chemicals Group Litigation v Gower Chemicals Ltd* [2008] EWHC 735 (QB), LTL 1/5/2008.   **68.30**

AMOUNT TO BE ALLOWED

London solicitors

Instructing specialist London solicitors for a complex personal injuries claim against the   **68.42**
police was regarded as unreasonable for a Sheffield-based claim in *A v Chief Constable of South Yorkshire* [2008] EWHC 1658 (QB), LTL 24/7/2008, applying *Wraith v Sheffield Forgemasters Ltd* [1998] 1 WLR 132.

A party will not recover costs which are duplicated by instructing two firms of solicitors, even if the second firm is based overseas in a claim with an international dimension (*Bühler AG v FP Spomax SA* [2008] EWHC 1109 (Pat), LTL 7/7/2008).

CONDITIONAL FEE AGREEMENTS

Recovering additional liabilities from the paying party

In *Crane v Canons Leisure Centre* [2007] EWCA Civ 1352, [2008] 2 All ER 931, a collective CFA   **68.49**
defined base costs as 'charges for work done by or on behalf of the Solicitors which would have been payable if this agreement did not provide for a success fee, calculated on the basis of the fees allowable for that work in the court in which the [claim] in question is conducted or would be conducted if proceedings were to be issued'. The costs of the detailed assessment, which was actually conducted by costs consultants engaged by the solicitors, were held to be part of the solicitors' base costs, and to attract the success fee on the same footing as the base costs on the substantive claim.

Chapter 69   Arbitration Claims

CLAIMS UNDER THE ARBITRATION ACT 1996

Challenging the substantive jurisdiction of the tribunal

A challenge to the substantive jurisdiction of an arbitral tribunal under the Arbitration Act   **69.13**
1996, s. 67(1), requires the permission of the High Court (s. 67(4)). For the limited jurisdiction of the Court of Appeal to review a refusal of permission, see the cases discussed at **69.15** in this supplement.

Challenging an award for serious irregularity

69.14 Failing to ensure that experienced counsel understood a point taken by the other side is not a serious irregularity, unless the arbitrator was aware of the misunderstanding (*Bandwidth Shipping Corporation v Intaari* [2007] EWCA Civ 998, [2008] 1 All ER (Comm) 1015).

Applications for permission to appeal

69.15 PD 62, para. 12.3(3), does not say whether the reasons relied on by the respondent in opposing the grant of permission to appeal under the Arbitration Act 1996, s. 69, need to be points of law. This was considered in *CTI Group Inc. v Transclear SA (No. 2)* [2007] EWHC 2340 (Comm), [2008] 1 All ER (Comm) 203, by Field J at [13].

'Where the grounds on which a respondent to a s. 69 appeal relies for upholding an award have not been pronounced upon by the arbitral tribunal, the court will inevitably come to its own conclusions on those grounds which, in my view, must be based on a point or points law. It does not follow from [*Vitol SA v Norelf Ltd* [1996] AC 800] that because under the [Arbitration Act 1979] neither leave nor a certificate that the point of law was one of general public importance was required that a respondent can rely on points that are not points of law. And where, as here, the tribunal has rejected the grounds relied on, the respondent must in my judgment show that in doing so the tribunal erred in law so that, if any of the relevant findings are mixed findings of fact and law, there will only be an error of law if the finding fails the [*Edwards v Bairstow* [1956] AC 14] test that the tribunal misdirected itself or no tribunal properly instructed as to the relevant law could have come to the determination reached.'

The residuary discretion recognised by *CGU International Insurance plc v AstraZeneca Insurance Co. Ltd* [2006] EWCA Civ 1340, [2007] Bus LR 162, to review a judge's decision to refuse permission under the Arbitration Act 1996, s. 67(4), is strictly limited. It may be used where there has been procedural unfairness in the judge's decision, or if there has been a failure to engage with the arguments on the limited question of an appeal (*Kazakhstan v Istil Group Ltd (No. 2)* [2007] EWCA Civ 471, [2008] Bus LR 878). These limited rights of access to the courts to challenge an award are compliant with the ECHR, art. 6(1). The High Court judge in effect operates as a second tier appeal court, because under the Arbitration Act 1996 an objection to jurisdiction is normally made first to the arbitrators. It is therefore a proportionate and legitimate restriction to provide in most cases that the High Court judge, rather than the Court of Appeal, is the final appeal court (*Republic of Kazakhstan v Istil Group Ltd (No. 2)*).

Hearings

69.16 While arbitration claims are typically heard in private (CPR, r. 62.10(1)), appeals to the Court of Appeal are heard in public unless there is a special reason for sitting in private. Any application for privacy or anonymity should be supported by written evidence at the time the application is made (*C v D* [2007] EWCA Civ 1282, [2008] Bus LR 843).

Chapter 70 Alternative Dispute Resolution

ADJUDICATIVE ADR

Expert determination

70.6 Where the parties agree to having their dispute determined by an independent expert, the expert's decision is binding on the parties even if it is wrong. It would frustrate the commercial purpose of such an agreement to imply a term that the expert's decision could be set aside if the expert failed to abide by the rules of natural justice, or was biased or gave the appearance of bias, or was guilty of gross or obvious error or gave a perverse decision (*Bernhard*

Schulte GmbH & Co. KG v Nile Holdings Ltd [2004] EWHC 977 (Comm), [2004] 2 Lloyd's Rep 352; *Owen Pell Ltd v Bindi (London) Ltd* [2008] CILL 2605).

An independent expert is obliged to decide the matter referred to him by the parties, so that a determination that is outside his jurisdiction will be a nullity (*Owen Pell Ltd v Bindi (London) Ltd*).

Chapter 71   The Appeals System

DECISIONS SUSCEPTIBLE TO APPEAL

71.2 A person who was not a party to the proceedings in the lower court can be an 'appellant' for the purposes of CPR, r. 51.2(3)(d) (*George Wimpey UK Ltd v Tewkesbury Borough Council* [2008] EWCA Civ 12, [2008] 1 WLR 1649). In deciding whether to grant permission to appeal to such a person the court will take into account whether any application was made to join the person in the lower court, and whether the person has a real interest in the appeal.

PERMISSION TO APPEAL

Seeking permission

71.12 An appellant is under a duty to inform the Civil Appeals Office in writing of any facts affecting the giving or refusing of permission to appeal (*Walbrook Trustees (Jersey) Ltd v Fattal* [2008] EWCA Civ 427, LTL 11/3/2008). If such facts arise after permission is granted, the appellant should write to the Civil Appeals Office and seek directions.

Limiting the issues on granting permission

71.18 Where a party is given a choice between proceeding with an appeal on a limited basis, or starting a fresh claim, choosing to proceed with the appeal does not amount to an election, but does mean that starting a fresh claim will be an abuse of process (*Koshy v DEG-Deutsche Investitions- und Entwicklungsgesellschaft mbH* [2008] EWCA Civ 27, LTL 5/2/2008).

LODGING DOCUMENTS

Appeal bundles

71.24 300 pages is a good guide to not over-filling files (*Leofelis SA v Lonsdale Sports Ltd* [2008] EWCA Civ 640, *The Times*, 23 July 2008). In complex appeals, particularly where several related appeals are to proceed together, bundles may need to be put together in chronological files (with the documents usually identifying their original file numbers), even though this may not comply with the terms of PD 52. Agreement should be attempted between the parties, and, if achieved, a consent order should be sought from the deputy master or supervising Lord Justice, on paper (*Leofelis SA v Lonsdale Sports Ltd*).

AFTER PERMISSION TO APPEAL IS GIVEN

Court of Appeal listing

71.32 In addition, the Court of Appeal sits at various times at a number of provincial trial centres. Partly this is for the convenience of parties, but it also serves a number of wider public interest purposes relating to access to justice and informing the public and senior judiciary (purposes which can be traced back to Magna Carta 1215, ss. 17 and 18). There is great reluctance in breaking fixtures for hearings in provincial centres, even where counsel of choice is unavailable for such a hearing through being pre-booked (*Newport City Council v Charles* [2008] EWCA Civ 893, *The Times*, 29 July 2008).

Reopening appeals

71.51 Cases where it is alleged that an appeal decision has been obtained through a fraud perpetrated on the appeal court should, save in the most exceptional circumstances, be brought by way of fresh proceedings rather than through applying to reopen the appeal (*Jaffray v Society of Lloyd's* [2007] EWCA Civ 586, [2008] 1 WLR 75). Exceptional cases are those where there is incontestable, admissible, evidence of the fraud. In other cases the appeal court will not be equipped to undertake the necessary inquiry into the facts, and may find it difficult to give an immediate remedy.

Statutory appeals

71.53 Substantive appeals under the Osteopaths Act 1993 lie to the High Court under CPR, Part 52, and so do appeals against interim suspension orders pending resolution of substantive appeals. Unless the High Court forms the view that the substantive appeal is bound to succeed, it should be slow to allow an appeal against an interim suspension order because it will not be in a position to assess whether the decision was wrong within the meaning of r. 52.11(3)(a) (*Moody v General Osteopathic Council* [2007] EWHC 2518 (Admin), [2008] 2 All ER 532).

Chapter 72   Hearing of Appeals

REVIEW OF THE DECISION BELOW

Examples of substantial procedural irregularity

72.14 Arguments that the judge in the lower court was predisposed against the appellant, often because of previous decisions, are frequently made but there is rarely any material to support such an allegation (*Hicks v Russell Jones and Walker* [2008] EWCA Civ 340, LTL 3/3/2008).

Ladd v Marshall principles

72.16 *Ladd v Marshall* [1954] 1 WLR 1489 was applied in relation to an application to adduce new evidence on an appeal against the entry of summary judgment in *Cotton v Rickard Metals Inc.* [2008] EWHC 824 (QB), LTL 25/4/2008.

GENERAL POWERS VESTED IN THE APPEAL COURT

72.18 The power to 'refer any claim or issue for determination by the lower court' in CPR, r. 52.10(2)(b), is stated in general terms, and allows the court to refer back a point to the trial judge which is only contingently relevant in the present appeal (*Hicks v Russell Jones and Walker* [2007] EWCA Civ 844, [2008] 2 All ER 1089). How the judge deals with such a reference (such as with written submissions, or further evidence) is a matter for him. Where the appeal court refers such a question to the lower court for a supplementary judgment, permission to appeal may be set aside where the supplementary judgment results in the appeal having no real prospect of success (*Hicks v Russell Jones and Walker* [2008] EWCA Civ 340, LTL 3/3/2008).

In rare cases, the Court of Appeal has jurisdiction to take a point of general importance of its own motion which was not raised in the court below (*Bulale v Secretary of State for the Home Department* (2008) *The Times*, 25 July 2008).

Chapter 73   Appeals to the House of Lords

STEPS AFTER PRESENTATION OF THE APPEAL

Counsel briefed to appear in the House of Lords are expected to be present at and throughout the hearing. Hearings in the House of Lords take precedence over hearings in lower courts, and counsel should not ordinarily accept instructions to appear in the House of Lords on a hearing for a fixed date if they already have a conflicting engagement. If through unforeseen circumstances counsel will find it difficult or embarrassing to appear in the House of Lords they should write to the presiding Law Lord and seek leave to be absent. This will ordinarily be given if sufficient reason is shown. See Practice Statement (House of Lords: Appearance of Counsel) [2008] 1 WLR 1143. **73.8**

Chapter 74   Judicial Review

BODIES OPEN TO JUDICIAL REVIEW

Central government and statutory bodies

A decision by a Crown Court judge not to make a compensation order under the Powers of Criminal Courts (Sentencing) Act 2000, s. 130, is a matter relating to trial on indictment. There is therefore no jurisdiction to seek judicial review of such a decision by virtue of the Supreme Court Act 1981, s. 29(3) (*R (Faithfull) v Crown Court at Ipswich* [2007] EWHC 2763 (Admin), [2008] 1 WLR 1636). Further, such lack of jurisdiction does not infringe the victim's rights under the European Convention on Human Rights, First Protocol, art. 1 (protection of property), in the Human Rights Act 1998, sch. 1 (see **99.33**), because the victim could bring a common law claim for damages against the defendant. **74.3**

PROCEDURE ONCE PERMISSION IS GRANTED

Interim applications

Practice Direction (Administrative Court: Uncontested Proceedings) [2008] 1 WLR 1377 **74.42**

The following practice direction replaces Practice Direction (Crown Office List: Consent Orders) [1997] 1 WLR 825.

1. Determination of proceedings

Where the parties are agreed as to the terms on which proceedings in the Administrative Court can be disposed of and require an order of the court to put those terms into effect they should lodge with the Administrative Court Office a document (with one copy thereof) signed by the parties setting out the terms of the proposed agreed order and a short statement of the matters relied on as justifying the making of the order, authorities and statutory provisions relied on being quoted.

The Administrative Court Office will then submit the document to the master or deputy master of the Crown Office and, if the court is satisfied that the order should be made, the order will be made without the need for attendance by the parties or their representatives. The making of the order will be publicised on the Court Service website.

If the court is not satisfied on the information originally provided or subsequently provided at the court's request, that the order can properly be made, the proceedings will be listed for hearing in the normal way.

2. Interim orders

Where the parties seek an interlocutory order and are agreed as to the terms of that proposed order they should lodge with the Administrative Court Office a document (with one copy thereof) signed by the parties setting out the terms of the proposed agreed order and a short statement of the matters relied on as justifying the making of the order, and, where appropriate, citing authorities and statutory provisions relied on.

The Administrative Court Office will then submit the document to the master or deputy master of the Crown Office and, if the court is satisfied that the order should be made, the order will be made without the need for attendance by the parties or their representatives.

3. Discontinuance/withdrawal of proceedings (including proceedings for habeas corpus)

(a) Where the parties are agreed that proceedings should be withdrawn but require the leave of the court to do so, or seek an order as to costs in relation to those proceedings, they should lodge with the Administrative Court Office a document (with one copy thereof) signed by the parties, setting out the terms of the proposed withdrawal. The order will be made in accordance with CPR, Part 40, without the need for attendance by the parties or their representatives. (The order will be entered and sealed by court staff. If one of the parties is a litigant in person, the Administrative Court Office will submit the proposed order to the master or deputy master of the Crown Office and, if the court is satisfied that the order should be made, the order will be made without the need for attendance by the parties or their representatives.) The court file will then be closed.

(b) Where leave of the court is not necessary for proceedings to be withdrawn and no order as to costs is sought, the claimant must inform the Administrative Court Office in writing, confirming that all other parties to the proceedings have been notified. The court file will then be closed.

(c) A claimant who files a notice of discontinuance of a claim under CPR, Part 38, must serve a copy of the notice on every other party to the proceedings. Unless the court orders otherwise, a claimant who discontinues is liable for the costs which a defendant against whom he discontinues incurred on or before the date on which notice of discontinuance was served on him. On receipt of a notice of discontinuance the court file will be closed.

(d) Where an appellant does not wish to pursue an appeal, he may request the court for an order that the appeal be dismissed; the request must contain a statement that the appellant is not a child or protected party. If such a request is granted, it will usually be on the basis that the appellant pays the costs of the appeal. If the appellant wishes to have the application or appeal dismissed without costs, the request must be accompanied by a consent signed by the respondent or his legal representative stating that the respondent is not a child or protected party and that he consents to the dismissal of the appeal without costs.

Chapter 76   Enforcement

INFORMATION AGAINST JUDGMENT DEBTORS

The expression 'an officer of that body' in CPR, Part 71, includes a director of the judgment debtor, but not a director of a corporate director of the judgment debtor (*Masri v Consolidated Contractors International Co. SAL* [2008] EWCA Civ 876, LTL 28/7/2008).

CHARGING ORDERS

An application for a charging order under the Solicitors Act 1974, s. 73, is not precluded by **76.21** the standard restriction in Precedent L (PD 43–48, para. 56.3) or the Solicitors Act 1974, s. 70(2)(b), precluding proceedings to enforce a solicitor's bill until detailed assessment proceedings are concluded (*Mastercigars Direct Ltd v Withers LLP* [2007] EWHC 2733 (Ch), [2008] 3 All ER 417).

RECEIVERS BY WAY OF EQUITABLE EXECUTION

Nature of receivership

An appointment of a receiver by way of equitable execution operates *in personam*, so the **76.33** extra-territorial restrictions relating to applications for third-party debt orders (for which see **76.16**) do not apply (*Masri v Consolidated Contractors International UK Ltd (No 2)* [2008] EWCA Civ 303, [2008] 2 Lloyd's Rep 128).

Chapter 77   Enforcement of Foreign Judgments

ENFORCEMENT IN ENGLAND AND WALES OF EUROPEAN ENFORCEMENT ORDERS

As from 1 October 2008, the references to particular types of enforcement in CPR, **77.24** r. 74.31(2), are removed by the Civil Procedure (Amendment) Rules 2008 (SI 2008/2178). Under the new rule, the requirement for a certificate of the sterling equivalent of the judgment sum applies to all applications to enforce EEOs expressed in a foreign currency. There are also technical amendments to r. 7.34 to clarify the principle that all enforcement proceedings under an EEO shall cease upon service on affected persons of an order under the EEO Regulation, art. 21(1).

Chapter 89   Secure Tenancies under the Housing Act 1985

EXTENDED DISCRETION AS TO THE TERMS OF ORDERS

Lewisham London Borough Council v Malcolm [2007] EWCA Civ 763, [2008] Ch 129, has been **89.53** reversed by the House of Lords [2008] UKHL 43, [2008] 3 WLR 194.

Chapter 94   Anti-social Behaviour and Harassment

DRINKING BANNING ORDERS

94.25 As a result of the delayed implementation of the drinking banning orders provisions of the
to Violent Crime Reduction Act 2006, CPR, rr. 65.31 to 65.36, have been deleted with effect
94.30 from 1 October 2008 (Civil Procedure (Amendment) Rules 2008 (SI 2008/2178), r. 36).
PD 65, paras 15.1 and 15.2, have also been deleted.

Chapter 99   Human Rights and Civil Procedure

ARTICLES OF THE CONVENTION INCORPORATED INTO THE HUMAN RIGHTS ACT 1998

Article 6: right to a fair trial

99.21 **Rights protected by article 6**   A challenge to the substantive jurisdiction of an arbitral
tribunal under the Arbitration Act 1996, s. 67(1), requires the permission of the High Court
(s. 67(4)). Subject to a limited residuary discretion recognised by *CGU International Insurance plc
v AstraZeneca Insurance Co. Ltd* [2006] EWCA Civ 1340, [2007] Bus LR 162, this means that in most
cases a decision of the High Court judge to refuse permission is final. See **69.13** and **69.15**.
This limited right of access to the courts to challenge an arbitral award has been held by
Kazakhstan v Istil Group Ltd (No. 2) [2007] EWCA Civ 471, [2008] Bus LR 878, to be compliant with
the European Convention on Human Rights, art. 6(1), in the Human Rights Act 1998, sch.
1. The High Court judge in effect operates as a second-tier appeal court, because under the
Arbitration Act 1996 an objection to jurisdiction is normally made first to the arbitrators, so
it is a proportionate and legitimate restriction to provide in most cases that the High Court
judge, rather than the Court of Appeal, is the final appeal court (*Kazakhstan v Istil Group Ltd
(No. 2)*).

99.33 **Article 1 of the First Protocol: protection of property**   There is no judicial review of a
decision by a Crown Court judge not to make a compensation order under the Powers of
Criminal Courts (Sentencing) Act 2000, s. 130, because this is a matter relating to trial on
indictment (Supreme Court Act 1981, s. 29(3)). Such lack of jurisdiction does not infringe
the victim's rights under art. 1 of the First Protocol, because the victim could bring a
common law claim for damages against the defendant (*R (Faithfull) v Crown Court at Ipswich*
[2007] EWHC 2763 (Admin), [2008] 1 WLR 1636).

Supplement to Appendix 1
Civil Procedure Rules 1998 and Practice Directions

SI 2008/2178 is the Civil Procedure (Amendment) Rules 2008.

CPR Part 2   Application and Interpretation of the Rules

Amendment effective from: 1 October 2008. Source: SI 2008/2178, r. 3.

In rule 2.3(1), in the parenthesis below the definition of 'defendant's home court', for 'Rule 6.5' substitute 'Rule 6.23'.

PD 2B   Practice Direction — Allocation of Cases to Levels of Judiciary

Amendment effective from: 1 October 2008. Source: 47th Update.

In para. 8.1A:

(a) in sub-para. (1), after '(anti-social behaviour);' insert 'and';
(b) in sub-para. (2), for '(parenting orders); and' substitute '(parenting orders).'; and
(c) omit sub-para. (3).

CPR Part 3   The Court's Case Management Powers

Amendment effective from: 1 October 2008. Source: SI 2008/2178, r. 4.

In rule 3.7—

(a) in paragraph (4)(ii), for 'shall' substitute 'will';
(b) in the parenthesis below paragraph (4)(ii), after 'this rule' insert 'and contains provisions about when a costs order is deemed to have been made and applying for an order under section 194(3) of the Legal Services Act 2007';
(c) in paragraph (6)(b), for 'shall' substitute 'will'; and
(d) in paragraph (7), for 'shall' substitute 'will'.

PD 3D   Practice Direction — Mesothelioma Claims

Amendment effective from: 1 October 2008. Source: 47th Update.

(1) In para. 2:

(a) in the definition of 'standard interim payment', for 'set amounts for' substitute 'payment in respect of'; and

(b) after 'Head of Civil Justice.' insert 'The amount of this payment is currently £50,000.'.

(2) In para. 6.7:

(a) after 'and' insert 'will normally order that'; and

(b) after 'payment' omit 'to'.

PD 5B   Practice Direction — Electronic Communication and Filing of Documents

Amendment effective from: 1 October 2008. Source: 47th Update.

(1) In para. 3.3A omit 'he is'.

(2) For the second parenthesis below para. 3.3A substitute:

'(Rules 6.3(1)(d) and 6.20(1)(d) permit service by email in accordance with the relevant practice direction. Rule 6.23(6) and PD 6A, para. 4, set out the circumstances in which a party may serve a document by email.)'.

CPR Part 6   Service of Documents

Amendment effective from: 1 October 2008. Source: SI 2008/2178, r. 5 and sch. 1.

Part 6 is replaced by the following new Part 6.

CPR Part 6   Service of Documents

I SCOPE OF THIS PART AND INTERPRETATION

6.1 Part 6 rules about service apply generally

This Part applies to the service of documents, except where—
(a) another Part, any other enactment or a practice direction makes different provision; or
(b) the court orders otherwise.
(Other Parts, for example, Part 54 (Judicial Review) and Part 55 (Possession Claims) contain specific provisions about service.)

6.2 Interpretation

In this Part—
(a) 'bank holiday' means a bank holiday under the Banking and Financial Dealings Act 1971 in the part of the United Kingdom where service is to take place;
(b) 'business day' means any day except Saturday, Sunday, a bank holiday, Good Friday or Christmas Day;
(c) 'claim' includes petition and any application made before action or to commence proceedings and 'claim form', 'claimant' and 'defendant' are to be construed accordingly; and
(d) 'solicitor' includes other authorised litigators within the meaning of the Courts and Legal Services Act 1990.

II SERVICE OF THE CLAIM FORM IN THE JURISDICTION

6.3 Methods of service

(1) A claim form may be served by any of the following methods—
    (a) personal service in accordance with rule 6.5;
    (b) first class post, document exchange or other service which provides for delivery on the next business day, in accordance with Practice Direction A supplementing this Part;
    (c) leaving it at a place specified in rule 6.7, 6.8, 6.9 or 6.10;
    (d) fax or other means of electronic communication in accordance with Practice Direction A supplementing this Part; or

     (e) any method authorised by the court under rule 6.15.
(2) A company may be served—
     (a) by any method permitted under this Part; or
     (b) by any of the methods of service set out in the Companies Act 1985 or the Companies Act 2006.
(3) A limited liability partnership may be served—
     (a) by any method permitted under this Part; or
     (b) by any of the methods of service set out in section 725 of the Companies Act 1985.

6.4 Who is to serve the claim form

(1) The court will serve the claim form except where—
     (a) a rule or practice direction provides that the claimant must serve it;
     (b) the claimant notifies the court that the claimant wishes to serve it; or
     (c) the court orders or directs otherwise.
(2) Where the court is to serve the claim form, it is for the court to decide which method of service is to be used.
(3) Where the court is to serve the claim form, the claimant must, in addition to filing a copy for the court, provide a copy for each defendant to be served.
(4) Where the court has sent—
     (a) a notification of outcome of postal service to the claimant in accordance with rule 6.18; or
     (b) a notification of non-service by a bailiff in accordance with rule 6.19, the court will not try to serve the claim form again.

6.5 Personal service

(1) Where required by another Part, any other enactment, a practice direction or a court order, a claim form must be served personally.
(2) In other cases, a claim form may be served personally except—
     (a) where rule 6.7 applies; or
     (b) in any proceedings against the Crown.
(Part 54 contains provisions about judicial review claims and Part 66 contains provisions about Crown proceedings.)
(3) A claim form is served personally on—
     (a) an individual by leaving it with that individual;
     (b) a company or other corporation by leaving it with a person holding a senior position within the company or corporation; or
     (c) a partnership (where partners are being sued in the name of their firm) by leaving it with—
         (i) a partner; or
         (ii) a person who, at the time of service, has the control or management of the partnership business at its principal place of business.
(Practice Direction A supplementing this Part sets out the meaning of 'senior position'.)

6.6 Where to serve the claim form — general provisions

(1) The claim form must be served within the jurisdiction except where rule 6.11 applies or as provided by Section IV of this Part.
(2) The claimant must include in the claim form an address at which the defendant may be served. That address must include a full postcode, unless the court orders otherwise.
(Paragraph 2.4 of the practice direction supplementing Part 16 contains provisions about postcodes.)
(3) Paragraph (2) does not apply where an order made by the court under rule 6.15 (service by an alternative method or at an alternative place) specifies the place or method of service of the claim form.

6.7 Service of the claim form on a solicitor

Subject to rule 6.5(1), where—
(a) the defendant has given in writing the business address within the jurisdiction of a solicitor as an address at which the defendant may be served with the claim form; or

(b) a solicitor acting for the defendant has notified the claimant in writing that the solicitor is instructed by the defendant to accept service of the claim form on behalf of the defendant at a business address within the jurisdiction,

the claim form must be served at the business address of that solicitor.

('Solicitor' has the extended meaning set out in rule 6.2(d).)

6.8 Service of the claim form where the defendant gives an address at which the defendant may be served

Subject to rules 6.5(1) and 6.7—

(a) the defendant may be served with the claim form at an address within the jurisdiction which the defendant has given for the purpose of being served with the proceedings; or

(b) in any claim by a tenant against a landlord, the claim form may be served at an address given by the landlord under section 48 of the Landlord and Tenant Act 1987.

6.9 Service of the claim form where the defendant does not give an address at which the defendant may be served

(1) This rule applies where—

    (a) rule 6.5(1) (personal service);

    (b) rule 6.7 (service of claim form on solicitor); and

    (c) rule 6.8 (defendant gives address at which the defendant may be served),

do not apply and the claimant does not wish to effect personal service under rule 6.5(2).

(2) Subject to paragraphs (3) to (6), the claim form must be served on the defendant at the place shown in the following table.

Nature of defendant to be served	Place of service
1. Individual	Usual or last known residence.
2. Individual being sued in the name of a business	Usual or last known residence of the individual; or principal or last known place of business.
3. Individual being sued in the business name of a partnership	Usual or last known residence of the individual; or principal or last known place of business of the partnership.
4. Limited liability partnership	Principal office of the partnership; or any place of business of the partnership within the jurisdiction which has a real connection with the claim.
5. Corporation (other than a company) incorporated in England and Wales	Principal office of the corporation; or any place within the jurisdiction where the corporation carries on its activities and which has a real connection with the claim.
6. Company registered in England and Wales	Principal office of the company; or any place of business of the company within the jurisdiction which has a real connection with the claim.
7. Any other company or corporation	Any place within the jurisdiction where the corporation carries on its activities; or any place of business of the company within the jurisdiction.

(3) Where a claimant has reason to believe that the address of the defendant referred to in entries 1, 2 or 3 in the table in paragraph (2) is an address at which the defendant no longer resides or carries on business, the claimant must take reasonable steps to ascertain the address of the defendant's current residence or place of business ('current address').

(4) Where, having taken the reasonable steps required by paragraph (3), the claimant—

    (a) ascertains the defendant's current address, the claim form must be served at that address; or

    (b) is unable to ascertain the defendant's current address, the claimant must consider whether there is—

        (i) an alternative place where; or

        (ii) an alternative method by which,

    service may be effected.

(5) If, under paragraph (4)(b), there is such a place where or a method by which service may be effected, the claimant must make an application under rule 6.15.

(6) Where paragraph (3) applies, the claimant may serve on the defendant's usual or last known address in accordance with the table in paragraph (2) where the claimant—
   (a) cannot ascertain the defendant's current residence or place of business; and
   (b) cannot ascertain an alternative place or an alternative method under paragraph (4)(b).

6.10 Service of the claim form in proceedings against the Crown

In proceedings against the Crown—
(a) service on the Attorney General must be effected on the Treasury Solicitor; and
(b) service on a government department must be effected on the solicitor acting for that department.
(The practice direction supplementing Part 66 gives the list published under section 17 of the Crown Proceedings Act 1947 of the solicitors acting in civil proceedings (as defined in that Act) for the different government departments on whom service is to be effected, and of their addresses.)

6.11 Service of the claim form by contractually agreed method

(1) Where—
   (a) a contract contains a term providing that, in the event of a claim being started in relation to the contract, the claim form may be served by a method or at a place specified in the contract; and
   (b) a claim solely in respect of that contract is started, the claim form may, subject to paragraph (2), be served on the defendant by the method or at the place specified in the contract.

(2) Where in accordance with the contract the claim form is to be served out of the jurisdiction, it may be served—
   (a) if permission to serve it out of the jurisdiction has been granted under rule 6.36; or
   (b) without permission under rule 6.32 or 6.33.

6.12 Service of the claim form relating to a contract on an agent of a principal who is out of the jurisdiction

(1) The court may, on application, permit a claim form relating to a contract to be served on the defendant's agent where —
   (a) the defendant is out of the jurisdiction;
   (b) the contract to which the claim relates was entered into within the jurisdiction with or through the defendant's agent; and
   (c) at the time of the application either the agent's authority has not been terminated or the agent is still in business relations with the defendant.

(2) An application under this rule—
   (a) must be supported by evidence setting out—
      (i) details of the contract and that it was entered into within the jurisdiction or through an agent who is within the jurisdiction;
      (ii) that the principal for whom the agent is acting was, at the time the contract was entered into and is at the time of the application, out of the jurisdiction;
      and
      (iii) why service out of the jurisdiction cannot be effected; and
   (b) may be made without notice.

(3) An order under this rule must state the period within which the defendant must respond to the particulars of claim.

(4) Where the court makes an order under this rule—
   (a) a copy of the application notice and the order must be served with the claim form on the agent; and
   (b) unless the court orders otherwise, the claimant must send to the defendant a copy of the application notice, the order and the claim form.

(5) This rule does not exclude the court's power under rule 6.15 (service by an alternative method or at an alternative place).

6.13 Service of the claim form on children and protected parties

(1) Where the defendant is a child who is not also a protected party, the claim form must be served on—
    (a) one of the child's parents or guardians; or
    (b) if there is no parent or guardian, an adult with whom the child resides or in whose care the child is.

(2) Where the defendant is a protected party, the claim form must be served on—
    (a) one of the following persons with authority in relation to the protected party as—
        (i) the attorney under a registered enduring power of attorney;
        (ii) the donee of a lasting power of attorney; or
        (iii) the deputy appointed by the Court of Protection; or
    (b) if there is no such person, an adult with whom the protected party resides or in whose care the protected party is.

(3) Any reference in this Section to a defendant or a party to be served includes the person to be served with the claim form on behalf of a child or protected party under paragraph (1) or (2).

(4) The court may make an order permitting a claim form to be served on a child or protected party, or on a person other than the person specified in paragraph (1) or (2).

(5) An application for an order under paragraph (4) may be made without notice.

(6) The court may order that, although a claim form has been sent or given to someone other than the person specified in paragraph (1) or (2), it is to be treated as if it had been properly served.

(7) This rule does not apply where the court has made an order under rule 21.2(3) allowing a child to conduct proceedings without a litigation friend.

(Part 21 contains rules about the appointment of a litigation friend and 'child' and 'protected party' have the same meaning as in rule 21.1.)

6.14 Deemed service

A claim form served in accordance with this Part is deemed to be served on the second business day after completion of the relevant step under rule 7.5(1).

6.15 Service of the claim form by an alternative method or at an alternative place

(1) Where it appears to the court that there is a good reason to authorise service by a method or at a place not otherwise permitted by this Part, the court may make an order permitting service by an alternative method or at an alternative place.

(2) On an application under this rule, the court may order that steps already taken to bring the claim form to the attention of the defendant by an alternative method or at an alternative place is good service.

(3) An application for an order under this rule—
    (a) must be supported by evidence; and
    (b) may be made without notice.

(4) An order under this rule must specify—
    (a) the method or place of service;
    (b) the date on which the claim form is deemed served; and
    (c) the period for—
        (i) filing an acknowledgment of service;
        (ii) filing an admission; or
        (iii) filing a defence.

6.16 Power of court to dispense with service of the claim form

(1) The court may dispense with service of a claim form in exceptional circumstances.

(2) An application for an order to dispense with service may be made at any time and—
    (a) must be supported by evidence; and
    (b) may be made without notice.

6.17 Notice and certificate of service relating to the claim form

(1) Where the court serves a claim form, the court will send to the claimant a notice which will include the date on which the claim form is deemed served under rule 6.14.

(2) Where the claimant serves the claim form, the claimant—

(a) must file a certificate of service within 21 days of service of the particulars of claim, unless all the defendants to the proceedings have filed acknowledgments of service within that time; and

(b) may not obtain judgment in default under Part 12 unless a certificate of service has been filed.

(3) The certificate of service must state—

(a) where rule 6.7, 6.8, 6.9 or 6.10 applies, the category of address at which the claimant believes the claim form has been served; and

(b) the details set out in the following table.

Method of service	Details to be certified
1. Personal service	Date of personal service.
2. First class post, document exchange or other service which provides for delivery on the next business day	Date of posting, or leaving with, delivering to or collection by the relevant service provider.
3. Delivery of document to or leaving it at a permitted place	Date when the document was delivered to or left at the permitted place.
4. Fax	Date of completion of the transmission.
5. Other electronic method	Date of sending the e-mail or other electronic transmission.
6. Alternative method or place	As required by the court.

6.18 Notification of outcome of postal service by the court

(1) Where—

(a) the court serves the claim form by post; and

(b) the claim form is returned to the court, the court will send notification to the claimant that the claim form has been returned.

(2) The claim form will be deemed to be served unless the address for the defendant on the claim form is not the relevant address for the purpose of rules 6.7 to 6.10.

6.19 Notice of non-service by bailiff

Where—

(a) the court bailiff is to serve a claim form; and

(b) the bailiff is unable to serve it on the defendant, the court will send notification to the claimant.

III   SERVICE OF DOCUMENTS OTHER THAN THE CLAIM FORM IN THE UNITED KINGDOM

6.20 Methods of service

(1) A document may be served by any of the following methods—

(a) personal service, in accordance with rule 6.22;

(b) first class post, document exchange or other service which provides for delivery on the next business day, in accordance with Practice Direction A supplementing this Part;

(c) leaving it at a place specified in rule 6.23;

(d) fax or other means of electronic communication in accordance with Practice Direction A supplementing this Part; or

(e) any method authorised by the court under rule 6.27.

(2) A company may be served—

(a) by any method permitted under this Part; or

   (b) by any of the methods of service set out in the Companies Act 1985 or the Companies Act 2006.

(3) A limited liability partnership may be served—
   (a) by any method permitted under this Part; or
   (b) by any of the methods of service set out in section 725 of the Companies Act 1985.

6.21 Who is to serve

(1) A party to proceedings will serve a document which that party has prepared except where—
   (a) a rule or practice direction provides that the court will serve the document; or
   (b) the court orders otherwise.
(2) The court will serve a document which it has prepared except where—
   (a) a rule or practice direction provides that a party must serve the document;
   (b) the party on whose behalf the document is to be served notifies the court that the party wishes to serve it; or
   (c) the court orders otherwise.
(3) Where the court is to serve a document, it is for the court to decide which method of service is to be used.
(4) Where the court is to serve a document prepared by a party, that party must provide a copy for the court and for each party to be served.

6.22 Personal service

(1) Where required by another Part, any other enactment, a practice direction or a court order, a document must be served personally.
(2) In other cases, a document may be served personally except—
   (a) where the party to be served has given an address for service under rule 6.23(2)(a); or
   (b) in any proceedings by or against the Crown.
(3) A document may be served personally as if the document were a claim form in accordance with rule 6.5(3).

6.23 Address for service

(1) A party to proceedings must give an address at which that party may be served with documents relating to those proceedings. The address must include a full postcode unless the court orders otherwise.
(Paragraph 2.4 of the practice direction supplementing Part 16 contains provisions about postcodes.)
(2) A party's address for service must be—
   (a) the business address within the United Kingdom of a solicitor acting for the party to be served; or
   (b) where there is no solicitor acting for the party to be served, an address within the United Kingdom at which the party resides or carries on business.
(3) Where there is no solicitor acting for the party to be served and the party does not have an address within the United Kingdom at which that party resides or carries on business, the party must give an address for service within the United Kingdom.
(Part 42 contains provisions about change of solicitor. Rule 42.1 provides that where a party gives the business address of a solicitor as that party's address for service, that solicitor will be considered to be acting for the party until the provisions of Part 42 are complied with.)
(4) Any document to be served in proceedings must be sent or transmitted to, or left at, the party's address for service under paragraph (2) or (3) unless it is to be served personally or the court orders otherwise.
(5) Where, in accordance with Practice Direction A supplementing this Part, a party indicates or is deemed to have indicated that they will accept service by fax, the fax number given by that party must be at the address for service.
(6) Where a party indicates in accordance with Practice Direction A supplementing this Part that they will accept service by electronic means other than fax, the e-mail address or electronic identification given by that party will be deemed to be at the address for service.

(7) In proceedings by or against the Crown, service of any document in the proceedings on the Crown must be effected in the same manner prescribed in rule 6.10 as if the document were a claim form.

(8) This rule does not apply where an order made by the court under rule 6.27 (service by an alternative method or at an alternative place) specifies where a document may be served.

6.24 Change of address for service

Where the address for service of a party changes, that party must give notice in writing of the change as soon as it has taken place to the court and every other party.

6.25 Service on children and protected parties

(1) An application for an order appointing a litigation friend where a child or protected party has no litigation friend must be served in accordance with rule 21.8(1) and (2).

(2) Any other document which would otherwise be served on a child or a protected party must be served on the litigation friend conducting the proceedings on behalf of the child or protected party.

(3) The court may make an order permitting a document to be served on the child or protected party or on some person other than the person specified in rule 21.8 or paragraph (2).

(4) An application for an order under paragraph (3) may be made without notice.

(5) The court may order that, although a document has been sent or given to someone other than the person specified in rule 21.8 or paragraph (2), the document is to be treated as if it had been properly served.

(6) This rule does not apply where the court has made an order under rule 21.2(3) allowing a child to conduct proceedings without a litigation friend.

6.26 Deemed Service

A document, other than a claim form, served in accordance with these Rules or any relevant practice direction is deemed to be served on the day shown in the following table—

Method of service	Deemed date of service
1. First class post (or other service which provides for delivery on the next business day)	The second day after it was posted, left with, delivered to or collected by the relevant service provider provided that day is a business day; or if not, the next business day after that day.
2. Document exchange	The second day after it was left with, delivered to or collected by the relevant service provider provided that day is a business day; or if not, the next business day after that day.
3. Delivering the document to or leaving it at a permitted address	If it is delivered to or left at the permitted address on a business day before 4.30 p.m., on that day; or in any other case, on the next business day after that day.
4. Fax	If the transmission of the fax is completed on a business day before 4.30 p.m., on that day; or in any other case, on the next business day after the day on which it was transmitted.
5. Other electronic method	If the e-mail or other electronic transmission is sent on a business day before 4.30 p.m., on that day; or in any other case, on the next business day after the day on which it was sent.
6. Personal service	If the document is served personally before 4.30 p.m. on a business day, on that day; or in any other case, on the next business day after that day.

(Paragraphs 10.1 to 10.7 of Practice Direction A supplementing this Part contain examples of how the date of deemed service is calculated.)

6.27 Service by an alternative method or at an alternative place

Rule 6.15 applies to any document in the proceedings as it applies to a claim form and reference to the defendant in that rule is modified accordingly.

6.28 Power to dispense with service

(1) The court may dispense with service of any document which is to be served in the proceedings.

(2) An application for an order to dispense with service must be supported by evidence and may be made without notice.

6.29 Certificate of service

Where a rule, practice direction or court order requires a certificate of service, the certificate must state the details required by the following table—

Method of Service	Details to be certified
1. Personal service	Date and time of personal service.
2. First class post, document exchange or other service which provides for delivery on the next business day	Date of posting, or leaving with, delivering to or collection by the relevant service provider.
3. Delivery of document to or leaving it at a permitted place	Date and time of when the document was delivered to or left at the permitted place.
4. Fax	Date and time of completion of the transmission.
5. Other electronic method	Date and time of sending the e-mail or other electronic transmission.
6. Alternative method or place permitted by	As required by the court.

IV SERVICE OF THE CLAIM FORM AND OTHER DOCUMENTS OUT OF THE JURISDICTION

6.30 Scope of this Section

This Section contains rules about—

(a) service of the claim form and other documents out of the jurisdiction;

(b) when the permission of the court is required and how to obtain that permission; and

(c) the procedure for service.

('Jurisdiction' is defined in rule 2.3(1).)

6.31 Interpretation

For the purposes of this Section—

(a) 'the Hague Convention' means the Convention on the service abroad of judicial and extra-judicial documents in civil or commercial matters signed at the Hague on 15 November 1965;

(b) 'the 1982 Act' means the Civil Jurisdiction and Judgments Act 1982;

(c) 'Civil Procedure Convention' means the Brussels and Lugano Conventions (as defined in section 1(1) of the 1982 Act) and any other Convention (including the Hague Convention) entered into by the United Kingdom regarding service out of the jurisdiction;

(d) 'the Judgments Regulation' means Council Regulation (EC) No. 44/2001 of 22 December 2000 on jurisdiction and the recognition and enforcement of judgments in civil and commercial matters, as amended from time to time and as applied by the Agreement made on 19 October 2005 between the European Community and the Kingdom of Denmark on jurisdiction and the recognition and enforcement of judgments in civil and commercial matters;

(e) 'the Service Regulation' means Regulation (EC) No. 1393/2007 of the European Parliament and of the Council of 13 November 2007 on the service in the Member States of judicial and extrajudicial documents in civil or commercial matters (service of documents), and repealing

Council Regulation (EC) No. 1348/2000, as amended from time to time and as applied by the Agreement made on 19 October 2005 between the European Community and the Kingdom of Denmark on the service of judicial and extrajudicial documents on civil and commercial matters;

(f) 'Commonwealth State' means a state listed in Schedule 3 to the British Nationality Act 1981;

(g) 'Contracting State' has the meaning given by section 1(3) of the 1982 Act;

(h) 'Convention territory' means the territory or territories of any Contracting State to which the Brussels or Lugano Conventions (as defined in section 1(1) of the 1982 Act) apply; and

(i) 'domicile' is to be determined—

  (i) in relation to a Convention territory, in accordance with sections 41 to 46 of the 1982 Act; and

  (ii) in relation to a Member State, in accordance with the Judgments Regulation and paragraphs 9 to 12 of Schedule 1 to the Civil Jurisdiction and Judgments Order 2001.

6.32 Service of the claim form where the permission of the court is not required — Scotland and Northern Ireland

(1) The claimant may serve the claim form on a defendant in Scotland or Northern Ireland where each claim made against the defendant to be served and included in the claim form is a claim which the court has power to determine under the 1982 Act and—

  (a) no proceedings between the parties concerning the same claim are pending in the courts of any other part of the United Kingdom; and

  (b) (i) the defendant is domiciled in the United Kingdom;

    (ii) the proceedings are within paragraph 11 of Schedule 4 to the 1982 Act; or

    (iii) the defendant is a party to an agreement conferring jurisdiction, within paragraph 12 of Schedule 4 to the 1982 Act.

(2) The claimant may serve the claim form on a defendant in Scotland or Northern Ireland where each claim made against the defendant to be served and included in the claim form is a claim which the court has power to determine under any enactment other than the 1982 Act notwithstanding that—

  (a) the person against whom the claim is made is not within the jurisdiction; or

  (b) the facts giving rise to the claim did not occur within the jurisdiction.

6.33 Service of the claim form where the permission of the court is not required — out of the United Kingdom

(1) The claimant may serve the claim form on a defendant out of the United Kingdom where each claim made against the defendant to be served and included in the claim form is a claim which the court has power to determine under the 1982 Act and—

  (a) no proceedings between the parties concerning the same claim are pending in the courts of any other part of the United Kingdom or any other Convention territory; and

  (b) (i) the defendant is domiciled in the United Kingdom or in any Convention territory;

    (ii) the proceedings are within article 16 of Schedule 1 or article 16 of Schedule 3C to the 1982 Act ; or

    (iii) the defendant is a party to an agreement conferring jurisdiction, within article 17 of Schedule 1 or article 17 of Schedule 3C to the 1982 Act.

(2) The claimant may serve the claim form on a defendant out of the United Kingdom where each claim made against the defendant to be served and included in the claim form is a claim which the court has power to determine under the Judgments Regulation and—

  (a) no proceedings between the parties concerning the same claim are pending in the courts of any other part of the United Kingdom or any other Member State; and

  (b) (i) the defendant is domiciled in the United Kingdom or in any Member State;

    (ii) the proceedings are within article 22 of the Judgments Regulation; or

    (iii) the defendant is a party to an agreement conferring jurisdiction, within article 23 of the Judgments Regulation.

(3) The claimant may serve the claim form on a defendant out of the United Kingdom where each claim made against the defendant to be served and included in the claim form is a claim which

the co urt has power to determine other than under the 1982 Act or the Judgments Regulation, notwithstanding that—

(a) the person against whom the claim is made is not within the jurisdiction; or

(b) the facts giving rise to the claim did not occur within the jurisdiction.

6.34 Notice of statement of grounds where the permission of the court is not required for service

(1) Where the claimant intends to serve a claim form on a defendant under rule 6.32 or 6.33, the claimant must—

(a) file with the claim form a notice containing a statement of the grounds on which the claimant is entitled to serve the claim form out of the jurisdiction; and

(b) serve a copy of that notice with the claim form.

(2) Where the claimant fails to file with the claim form a copy of the notice referred to in paragraph (1)(a), the claim form may only be served—

(a) once the claimant files the notice; or

(b) if the court gives permission.

6.35 Period for responding to the claim form where permission was not required for service

(1) This rule sets out the period for—

(a) filing an acknowledgment of service;

(b) filing an admission; or

(c) filing a defence,

where a claim form has been served out of the jurisdiction under rule 6.32 or 6.33.

(Part 10 contains rules about acknowledgments of service, Part 14 contains rules about admissions and Part 15 contains rules about defences.)

Service of the claim form on a defendant in Scotland or Northern Ireland

(2) Where the claimant serves on a defendant in Scotland or Northern Ireland under rule 6.32, the period—

(a) for filing an acknowledgment of service or admission is 21 days after service of the particulars of claim; or

(b) for filing a defence is—

(i) 21 days after service of the particulars of claim; or

(ii) where the defendant files an acknowledgment of service, 35 days after service of the particulars of claim.

(Part 7 provides that particulars of claim must be contained in or served with the claim form or served separately on the defendant within 14 days after service of the claim form.)

Service of the claim form on a defendant in a Convention territory within Europe or a Member State

(3) Where the claimant serves the claim form on a defendant in a Convention territory within Europe or a Member State under rule 6.33, the period—

(a) for filing an acknowledgment of service or admission, is 21 days after service of the particulars of claim; or

(b) for filing a defence is—

(i) 21 days after service of the particulars of claim; or

(ii) where the defendant files an acknowledgment of service, 35 days after service of the particulars of claim.

Service of the claim form on a defendant in a Convention territory outside Europe

(4) Where the claimant serves the claim form on a defendant in a Convention territory outside Europe under rule 6.33, the period—

(a) for filing an acknowledgment of service or admission, is 31 days after service of the particulars of claim; or

(b) for filing a defence is—

(i) 31 days after service of the particulars of claim; or

(ii) where the defendant files an acknowledgment of service, 45 days after service of the particulars of claim.

Service on a defendant elsewhere

(5) Where the claimant serves the claim form under rule 6.33 in a country not referred to in paragraph (3) or (4), the period for responding to the claim form is set out in Practice Direction B supplementing this Part.

6.36 Service of the claim form where the permission of the court is required

In any proceedings to which rule 6.32 or 6.33 does not apply, the claimant may serve a claim form out of the jurisdiction with the permission of the court if any of the grounds set out in paragraph 3.1 of Practice Direction B supplementing this Part apply.

6.37 Application for permission to serve the claim form out of the jurisdiction

(1) An application for permission under rule 6.36 must set out—
  (a) which ground in paragraph 3.1 of Practice Direction B supplementing this Part is relied on;
  (b) that the claimant believes that the claim has a reasonable prospect of success; and
  (c) the defendant's address or, if not known, in what place the defendant is, or is likely, to be found.
(2) Where the application is made in respect of a claim referred to in paragraph 3.1(3) of Practice Direction B supplementing this Part, the application must also state the grounds on which the claimant believes that there is between the claimant and the defendant a real issue which it is reasonable for the court to try.
(3) The court will not give permission unless satisfied that England and Wales is the proper place in which to bring the claim.
(4) In particular, where—
  (a) the application is for permission to serve a claim form in Scotland or Northern Ireland; and
  (b) it appears to the court that the claimant may also be entitled to a remedy in Scotland or Northern Ireland, the court, in deciding whether to give permission, will—
    (i)   compare the cost and convenience of proceeding there or in the jurisdiction; and
    (ii) (where relevant) have regard to the powers and jurisdiction of the Sheriff court in Scotland or the county courts or courts of summary jurisdiction in Northern Ireland.
(5) Where the court gives permission to serve a claim form out of the jurisdiction—
  (a) it will specify the periods within which the defendant may—
    (i)   file an acknowledgment of service;
    (ii) file or serve an admission;
    (iii) file a defence; or
    (iv) file any other response or document required by a rule in another Part, any other enactment or a practice direction; and
  (b) it may—
    (i)   give directions about the method of service; and
    (ii) give permission for other documents in the proceedings to be served out of the jurisdiction.
(The periods referred to in paragraphs (5)(a)(i), (ii) and (iii) are those specified in the Table in Practice Direction B supplementing this Part.)

6.38 Service of documents other than the claim form — permission

(1) Unless paragraph (2) or (3) applies, where the permission of the court is required for the claimant to serve the claim form out of the jurisdiction, the claimant must obtain permission to serve any other document in the proceedings out of the jurisdiction.
(2) Where—
  (a) the court gives permission for a claim form to be served on a defendant out of the jurisdiction; and
  (b) the claim form states that particulars of claim are to follow, the permission of the court is not required to serve the particulars of claim.
(3) The permission of the court is not required if a party has given an address for service in Scotland or Northern Ireland.

6.39 Service of application notice on a non-party to the proceedings

(1) Where an application notice is to be served out of the jurisdiction on a person who is not a party to the proceedings rules 6.35 and 6.37(5)(a)(i), (ii) and (iii) do not apply.

(2) Where an application is served out of the jurisdiction on a person who is not a party to the proceedings, that person may make an application to the court under Part 11 as if that person were a defendant, but rule 11(2) does not apply.

(Part 11 contains provisions about disputing the court's jurisdiction.)

6.40 Methods of service — general provisions

(1) This rule contains general provisions about the method of service of a claim form or other document on a party out of the jurisdiction.

Where service is to be effected on a party in Scotland or Northern Ireland

(2) Where a party serves any document on a party in Scotland or Northern Ireland, it must be served by a method permitted by Section II (and references to 'jurisdiction' in that Section are modified accordingly) or Section III of this Part and rule 6.23(4) applies.

Where service is to be effected on a defendant out of the United Kingdom

(3) Where the claimant wishes to serve a claim form or any other document on a defendant out of the United Kingdom, it may be served—
 (a) by any method provided for by—
  (i) rule 6.41 (service in accordance with the Service Regulation);
  (ii) rule 6.42 (service through foreign governments, judicial authorities and British Consular authorities); or
  (iii) rule 6.44 (service of claim form or other document on a State);
 (b) by any method permitted by a Civil Procedure Convention; or
 (c) by any other method permitted by the law of the country in which it is to be served.

(4) Nothing in paragraph (3) or in any court order authorises or requires any person to do anything which is contrary to the law of the country where the claim form or other document is to be served.

(A list of the countries with whom the United Kingdom has entered into a Civil Procedure Convention, and a link to the relevant Convention, may be found on the Foreign and Commonwealth Office website at—

<http://www.fco.gov.uk/en/about-the-fco/publications/treaties/lists-treaties/bilateral-civilprocedure)>

6.41 Service in accordance with the Service Regulation

(1) This rule applies where the claimant wishes to serve the claim form or other document in accordance with the Service Regulation.

(2) The claimant must file—
 (a) the claim form or other document;
 (b) any translation; and
 (c) any other documents required by the Service Regulation.

(3) When the claimant files the documents referred to in paragraph (2), the court officer will—
 (a) seal(GL) the copy of the claim form; and
 (b) forward the documents to the Senior Master.

(4) Rule 6.47 does not apply to this rule.

(The Service Regulation is annexed to Practice Direction B supplementing this Part.)

(Article 20(1) of the Service Regulation provides that the Regulation prevails over other provisions contained in any other agreement or arrangement concluded by Member States.)

6.42 Service through foreign governments, judicial authorities and British Consular authorities

(1) Where the claimant wishes to serve a claim form or any other document on a defendant in any country which is a party to a Civil Procedure Convention providing for service in that country, it may be served—

    (a) through the authority designated under the Hague Convention (where relevant) in respect of that country; or

    (b) if the law of that country permits—

       (i) through the judicial authorities of that country, or

       (ii) through a British Consular authority in that country (subject to any provisions of the applicable convention about the nationality of persons who may be served by such a method).

(2) Where the claimant wishes to serve a claim form or any other document on a defendant in any country with respect to which there is no Civil Procedure Convention providing for service in that country, the claim form or other document may be served, if the law of that country so permits—

    (a) through the government of that country, where that government is willing to serve it; or

    (b) through a British Consular authority in that country.

(3) Where the claimant wishes to serve the claim form or other document in—

    (a) any Commonwealth State which is not a party to the Hague Convention;

    (b) the Isle of Man or the Channel Islands; or

    (c) any British overseas territory,

the methods of service permitted by paragraphs (1)(b) and (2) are not available and the claimant or the claimant's agent must effect service direct, unless Practice Direction B supplementing this Part provides otherwise.

(A list of British overseas territories is reproduced in paragraph 5.2 of Practice Direction B supplementing this Part.)

6.43 Procedure where service is to be through foreign governments, judicial authorities and British Consular authorities

(1) This rule applies where the claimant wishes to serve a claim form or any other document under rule 6.42(1) or 6.42(2).

(2) Where this rule applies, the claimant must file—

    (a) a request for service of the claim form or other document specifying one or more of the methods in rule 6.42(1) or 6.42(2);

    (b) a copy of the claim form or other document;

    (c) any other documents or copies of documents required by Practice Direction B supplementing this Part; and

    (d) any translation required under rule 6.45.

(3) Where the claimant files the documents specified in paragraph (2), the court officer will—

    (a) seal[(GL)] the copy of the claim form or other document; and

    (b) forward the documents to the Senior Master.

(4) The Senior Master will send documents forwarded under this rule—

    (a) where the claim form or other document is being served through the authority designated under the Hague Convention, to that authority; or

    (b) in any other case, to the Foreign and Commonwealth Office with a request that it arranges for the claim form or other document to be served.

(5) An official certificate which—

    (a) states that the method requested under paragraph (2)(a) has been performed and the date of such performance;

    (b) states, where more than one method is requested under paragraph (2)(a), which method was used; and

    (c) is made by—

       (i) a British Consular authority in the country where the method requested under paragraph (2)(a) was performed;

       (ii) the government or judicial authorities in that country; or

       (iii) the authority designated in respect of that country under the Hague Convention, is evidence of the facts stated in the certificate.

(6) A document purporting to be an official certificate under paragraph (5) is to be treated as such a certificate, unless it is proved not to be.

6.44 Service of claim form or other document on a State

(1) This rule applies where a claimant wishes to serve the claim form or other document on a State.
(2) In this rule, 'State' has the meaning given by section 14 of the State Immunity Act 1978.
(3) The claimant must file in the Central Office of the Royal Courts of Justice—
    (a) a request for service to be arranged by the Foreign and Commonwealth Office;
    (b) a copy of the claim form or other document; and
    (c) any translation required under rule 6.45.
(4) The Senior Master will send the documents filed under this rule to the Foreign and Commonwealth Office with a request that it arranges for them to be served.
(5) An official certificate by the Foreign and Commonwealth Office stating that a claim form has been duly served on a specified date in accordance with a request made under this rule is evidence of that fact.
(6) A document purporting to be such a certificate is to be treated as such a certificate, unless it is proved not to be.
(7) Where—
    (a) section 12(6) of the State Immunity Act 1978 applies; and
    (b) the State has agreed to a method of service other than through the Foreign and Commonwealth Office,
the claim form or other document may be served either by the method agreed or in accordance with this rule.
(Section 12(6) of the State Immunity Act 1978 provides that section 12(1) enables the service of a claim form or other document in a manner to which the State has agreed.)

6.45 Translation of claim form or other document

(1) Except where paragraph (4) or (5) applies, every copy of the claim form or other document filed under rule 6.43 (service through foreign governments, judicial authorities etc.) or 6.44 (service of claim form or other document on a State) must be accompanied by a translation of the claim form or other document.
(2) The translation must be—
    (a) in the official language of the country in which it is to be served; or
    (b) if there is more than one official language of that country, in any official language which is appropriate to the place in the country where the claim form or other document is to be served.
(3) Every translation filed under this rule must be accompanied by a statement by the person making it that it is a correct translation, and the statement must include that person's name, address and qualifications for making the translation.
(4) The claimant is not required to file a translation of a claim form or other document filed under rule 6.43 (service through foreign governments, judicial authorities etc.) where the claim form or other document is to be served—
    (a) in a country of which English is an official language; or
    (b) on a British citizen (within the meaning of the British Nationality Act 1981), unless a Civil Procedure Convention requires a translation.
(5) The claimant is not required to file a translation of a claim form or other document filed under rule 6.44 (service of claim form or other document on a State) where English is an official language of the State in which the claim form or other document is to be served.
(The Service Regulation contains provisions about the translation of documents.)

6.46 Undertaking to be responsible for expenses

Every request for service filed under rule 6.43 (service through foreign governments, judicial authorities etc.) or rule 6.44 (service of claim form or other document on a State) must contain an undertaking by the person making the request—
(a) to be responsible for all expenses incurred by the Foreign and Commonwealth Office or foreign judicial authority; and
(b) to pay those expenses to the Foreign and Commonwealth Office or foreign judicial authority on being informed of the amount.

6.47 Proof of service before obtaining judgment

Where—
(a) a hearing is fixed when the claim form is issued;
(b) the claim form is served on a defendant out of the jurisdiction; and
(c) that defendant does not appear at the hearing,
the claimant may not obtain judgment against the defendant until the claimant files written evidence that the claim form has been duly served in accordance with this Part.

V SERVICE OF DOCUMENTS FROM FOREIGN COURTS OR TRIBUNALS

6.48 Scope of this Section

This Section—
(a) applies to the service in England and Wales of any document in connection with civil or commercial proceedings in a foreign court or tribunal; but
(b) does not apply where the Service Regulation (which has the same meaning as in rule 6.31(e)) applies.

6.49 Interpretation

In this Section—
(a) 'convention country' means a country in relation to which there is a Civil Procedure Convention (which has the same meaning as in rule 6.31(c));
(b) 'foreign court or tribunal' means a court or tribunal in a country outside of the United Kingdom; and
(c) 'process server' means—
    (i) a process server appointed by the Lord Chancellor to serve documents to which this Section applies, or
    (ii) the process server's agent.

6.50 Request for service

The Senior Master will serve a document to which this Section applies upon receipt of—
(a) a written request for service—
    (i) where the foreign court or tribunal is in a convention country, from a consular or other authority of that country; or
    (ii) from the Secretary of State for Foreign and Commonwealth Affairs, with a recommendation that service should be effected;
(b) a translation of that request into English;
(c) two copies of the document to be served; and
(d) unless the foreign court or tribunal certifies that the person to be served understands the language of the document, two copies of a translation of it into English.

6.51 Method of service

The Senior Master will determine the method of service.

6.52 After service

(1) Where service of a document has been effected by a process server, the process server must—
    (a) send to the Senior Master a copy of the document, and
        (i) proof of service; or
        (ii) a statement why the document could not be served; and
    (b) if the Senior Master directs, specify the costs incurred in serving or attempting to serve the document.
(2) The Senior Master will send to the person who requested service—
    (a) a certificate, sealed with the seal of the Supreme Court for use out of the jurisdiction, stating—
        (i) when and how the document was served or the reason why it has not been served; and

(ii) where appropriate, an amount certified by a costs judge to be the costs of serving or attempting to serve the document; and

(b) a copy of the document.

PD 6   Practice Direction — Service

Amendment effective from: 1 October 2008. Source: 47th Update.
PD 6 is replaced by the following new PD 6A.

PD 6A   Practice Direction — Service within the United Kingdom

This practice direction supplements CPR, Part 6.

Scope of This Practice Direction

1.1 This Practice Direction supplements:
(1) Section II (service of the claim form in the jurisdiction) of Part 6;
(2) Section III (service of documents other than the claim form in the United Kingdom) of Part 6; and
(3) r. 6.40 in relation to the method of service on a party in Scotland or Northern Ireland.
(PD 6B contains provisions relevant to service on a party in Scotland or Northern Ireland, including provisions about service out of the jurisdiction where permission is and is not required and the period for responding to an application notice.)

When Service May Be by Document Exchange

2.1 Service by document exchange (DX) may take place only where:
(1) the address at which the party is to be served includes a numbered box at a DX, or
(2) the writing paper of the party who is to be served or of the solicitor acting for that party sets out a DX box number, and
(3) the party or the solicitor acting for that party has not indicated in writing that they are unwilling to accept service by DX.

How Service Is Effected by Post, an Alternative Service Provider or DX

3.1 Service by post, DX or other service which provides for delivery on the next business day is effected by:
(1) placing the document in a post box;
(2) leaving the document with or delivering the document to the relevant service provider; or
(3) having the document collected by the relevant service provider.

Service by Fax or Other Electronic Means

4.1 Subject to the provisions of r. 6.23(5) and (6), where a document is to be served by fax or other electronic means:
(1) the party who is to be served or the solicitor acting for that party must previously have indicated in writing to the party serving:
(a) that the party to be served or the solicitor is willing to accept service by fax or other electronic means; and
(b) the fax number, email address or other electronic identification to which it must be sent; and
(2) the following are to be taken as sufficient written indications for the purposes of para. 4.1(1):

(a) a fax number set out on the writing paper of the solicitor acting for the party to be served;

(b) an email address set out on the writing paper of the solicitor acting for the party to be served but only where it is stated that the email address may be used for service; or

(c) a fax number, email address or electronic identification set out on a statement of case or a response to a claim filed with the court.

4.2 Where a party intends to serve a document by electronic means (other than by fax) that party must first ask the party who is to be served whether there are any limitations to the recipient's agreement to accept service by such means (for example, the format in which documents are to be sent and the maximum size of attachments that may be received).

4.3 Where a document is served by electronic means, the party serving the document need not in addition send or deliver a hard copy.

Service on Members of the Regular Forces and United States Air Force

5.1 The provisions that apply to service on members of the regular forces (within the meaning of the Armed Forces Act 2006) and members of the United States Air Force are annexed to this practice direction.

Personal Service on a Company or Other Corporation

6.1 Personal service on a registered company or corporation in accordance with r. 6.5(3) is effected by leaving a document with a person holding a senior position.

6.2 Each of the following persons is a person holding a senior position:

(1) in respect of a registered company or corporation, a director, the treasurer, the secretary of the company or corporation, the chief executive, a manager or other officer of the company or corporation; and

(2) in respect of a corporation which is not a registered company, in addition to any of the persons set out in sub-para. (1), the mayor, the chairman, the president, a town clerk or similar officer of the corporation.

Certificate of Service Where Claimant Serves the Claim Form

7.1 Where, pursuant to r. 6.17(2), the claimant files a certificate of service, the claimant is not required to and should not file:

(1) a further copy of the claim form with the certificate of service; and

(2) a further copy of:

(a) the particulars of claim (where not included in the claim form); or

(b) any document attached to the particulars of claim,

with the certificate of service where that document has already been filed with the court.

(Rule 7.4 requires the claimant to file a copy of the particulars of claim (where served separately from the claim form) within seven days of service on the defendant.)

Service by the Court

8.1 Where the court serves a document in accordance with r. 6.4 or 6.21(2), the method will normally be first-class post.

8.2 Where the court serves a claim form, delivers a defence to a claimant or notifies a claimant that the defendant has filed an acknowledgment of service, the court will also serve or deliver a copy of any notice of funding that has been filed, if:

(1) it was filed at the same time as the claim form, defence or acknowledgment of service, and

(2) copies of it were provided for service.

(Rule 44.15 deals with the provision of information about funding arrangements.)

Application for an Order for Service by an Alternative Method or at an Alternative Place

9.1 Where an application for an order under r. 6.15 is made before the document is served, the application must be supported by evidence stating:

(1) the reason why an order is sought;

(2) what alternative method or place is proposed, and

(3) why the applicant believes that the document is likely to reach the person to be served by the method or at the place proposed.

9.2 Where the application for an order is made after the applicant has taken steps to bring the document to the attention of the person to be served by an alternative method or at an alternative place, the application must be supported by evidence stating:

(1) the reason why the order is sought;

(2) what alternative method or alternative place was used;

(3) when the alternative method or place was used; and

(4) why the applicant believes that the document is likely to have reached the person to be served by the alternative method or at the alternative place.

9.3 Examples:

(1) an application to serve by posting or delivering to an address of a person who knows the other party must be supported by evidence that if posted or delivered to that address, the document is likely to be brought to the attention of the other party;

(2) an application to serve by sending a SMS text message or leaving a voicemail message at a particular telephone number saying where the document is must be accompanied by evidence that the person serving the document has taken, or will take, appropriate steps to ensure that the party being served is using that telephone number and is likely to receive the message; and

(3) an application to serve by email to a company (where para. 4.1 does not apply) must be supported by evidence that the email address to which the document will be sent is one which is likely to come to the attention of a person holding a senior position in that company.

Deemed Service of a Document Other Than a Claim Form

10.1 Rule 6.26 contains provisions about deemed service of a document other than a claim form. Examples of how deemed service is calculated are set out below.

Example 1

10.2 Where the document is posted (by first-class post) on a Monday (a business day), the day of deemed service is the following Wednesday (a business day).

Example 2

10.3 Where the document is left in a numbered box at the DX on a Friday (a business day), the day of deemed service is the following Monday (a business day).

Example 3

10.4 Where the document is sent by fax on a Saturday and the transmission of that fax is completed by 4.30 p.m. on that day, the day of deemed service is the following Monday (a business day).

Example 4

10.5 Where the document is served personally before 4.30 p.m. on a Sunday, the day of deemed service is the next day (Monday, a business day).

Example 5

10.6 Where the document is delivered to a permitted address after 4.30 p.m. on the Thursday (a business day) before Good Friday, the day of deemed service is the following Tuesday (a business day) as the Monday is a bank holiday.

Example 6

10.7 Where the document is posted (by first-class post) on a bank holiday Monday, the day of deemed service is the following Wednesday (a business day).

ANNEX

SERVICE ON MEMBERS OF THE REGULAR FORCES

1. The following information is for litigants and legal representatives who wish to serve legal documents in civil proceedings in the courts of England and Wales on parties to the proceedings who are (or who, at the material time, were) members of the regular forces (as defined in the Armed Forces Act 2006).

2. The proceedings may take place in the county court or the High Court, and the documents to be served may be claim forms, interim application notices and pre-action application notices. Proceedings for divorce or maintenance and proceedings in the Family Courts generally are subject to special rules as to service which are explained in a practice direction issued by the Senior District Judge of the Principal Registry on 26 June 1979.

3. In this Annex, the person wishing to effect service is referred to as the 'claimant' and the member of the regular forces to be served is referred to as 'the member'; the expression 'overseas' means outside the United Kingdom.

Enquiries as to address

4. As a first step, the claimant's legal representative will need to find out where the member is serving, if this is not already known. For this purpose the claimant's legal representative should write to the appropriate officer of the Ministry of Defence as specified in para. 10 below.

5. The letter of enquiry should in every case show that the writer is a legal representative and that the enquiry is made solely with a view to the service of legal documents in civil proceedings.

6. In all cases the letter must give the full name, service number, rank or rate, and Ship, Arm or Trade, Regiment or Corps and Unit or as much of this information as is available. Failure to quote the service number and the rank or rate may result either in failure to identify the member or in considerable delay.

7. The letter must contain an undertaking by the legal representative that, if the address is given, it will be used solely for the purpose of issuing and serving documents in the proceedings and that so far as is possible the legal representative will disclose the address only to the court and not to the claimant or to any other person or body. A legal representative in the service of a public authority or private company must undertake that the address will be used solely for the purpose of issuing and serving documents in the proceedings and that the address will not be disclosed so far as is possible to any other part of the legal representative's employing organisation or to any other person but only to the court. Normally on receipt of the required information and undertaking the appropriate office will give the service address.

8. If the legal representative does not give the undertaking, the only information that will be given is whether the member is at that time serving in England or Wales, Scotland, Northern Ireland or overseas.

9. It should be noted that a member's address which ends with a British Forces Post Office address and reference (BFPO) will nearly always indicate that the member is serving overseas.

10. The letter of enquiry should be addressed as follows:

(a) *Royal Navy and Royal Marine Officers, Ratings and Other Ranks*
Director Naval Personnel
Fleet Headquarters
MP 3.1
Leach Building
Whale Island
Portsmouth
Hampshire
PO2 8BY

(b) *Army Officers and Other Ranks*
Army Personnel Centre
Disclosures 1
MP 520
Kentigern House
65 Brown Street
Glasgow G2 8EX

(c) *Royal Air Force Officers and Other Ranks*
Manning 22E
RAF Disclosures

Room 221B
Trenchard Hall
RAF Cranwell
Sleaford
Lincolnshire
NG34 8HB

Assistance in serving documents on members

11. Once the claimant's legal representative has ascertained the member's address, the legal representative may use that address as the address for service by post, in cases where this method of service is allowed by the Civil Procedure Rules. There are, however, some situations in which service of the proceedings, whether in the High Court or in the county court, must be effected personally; in these cases an appointment will have to be sought, through the Commanding Officer of the Unit, Establishment or Ship concerned, for the purpose of effecting service. The procedure for obtaining an appointment is described below, and it applies whether personal service is to be effected by the claimant's legal representative or the legal representative's agent or by a court bailiff, or, in the case of proceedings served overseas (with the leave of the court) through the British Consul or the foreign judicial authority.

12. The procedure for obtaining an appointment to effect personal service is by application to the Commanding Officer of the Unit, Establishment or Ship in which the member is serving. The Commanding Officer may grant permission for the document server to enter the Unit, Establishment or Ship but if this is not appropriate the Commanding Officer may offer arrangements for the member to attend at a place in the vicinity of the Unit, Establishment or Ship in order that the member may be served. If suitable arrangements cannot be made the legal representative will have evidence that personal service is impracticable, which may be useful in an application for service by an alternative method or at an alternative place.

General

13. Subject to the procedure outlined in paras 11 and 12, there are no special arrangements to assist in the service of legal documents when a member is outside the United Kingdom. The appropriate office will, however, give an approximate date when the member is likely to return to the United Kingdom.

14. It sometimes happens that a member has left the regular forces by the time an enquiry as to address is made. If the claimant's legal representative confirms that the proceedings result from an occurrence when the member was in the regular forces and the legal representative gives the undertaking referred to in para. 7, the last known private address after discharge will normally be provided. In no other case, however, will the Ministry of Defence disclose the private address of a member of the regular forces.

SERVICE ON MEMBERS OF UNITED STATES AIR FORCE

15. In addition to the information contained in the memorandum of 26 July 1979, and after some doubts having been expressed as to the correct procedure to be followed by persons having civil claims against members of the United States Air Force in England and Wales, the Lord Chancellor's Office (as it was then) issued the following notes for guidance with the approval of the appropriate United States authorities.

16. Instructions have been issued by the United States authorities to the commanding officers of all their units in England and Wales that every facility is to be given for the service of documents in civil proceedings on members of the United States Air Force. The proper course to be followed by a creditor or other person having a claim against a member of the United States Air Force is for that person to communicate with the commanding officer or, where the unit concerned has a legal officer, with the legal officer of the defendant's unit requesting the provision of facilities for the service of documents on the defendant. It is not possible for the United States authorities to act as arbitrators when a civil claim is made against a member of their forces. It is, therefore, essential that the claim should either be admitted by the defendant or judgment should be obtained on it, whether in the High Court or a county court. If a claim has been admitted or judgment has been obtained and the

claimant has failed to obtain satisfaction within a reasonable period, the claimant's proper course is then to write to: Office of the Staff Judge Advocate, Headquarters, Third Air Force, RAF Mildenhall, Suffolk, enclosing a copy of the defendant's written admission of the claim or, as the case may be, a copy of the judgment. Steps will then be taken by the Staff Judge Advocate to ensure that the matter is brought to the defendant's attention with a view to prompt satisfaction of the claim.

PD 6B   Practice Direction — Service Out of the Jurisdiction

Amendment effective from: 1 October 2008. Source: 47th Update.
PD 6B is replaced by the following new PD 6B.

PD 6B   Practice Direction — Service Out of the Jurisdiction

This practice direction supplements Section IV of CPR, Part 6.

Scope of This Practice Direction

1.1 This Practice Direction supplements Section IV (service of the claim form and other documents out of the jurisdiction) of Part 6.

(PD 6A contains relevant provisions supplementing r. 6.40 in relation to the method of service on a party in Scotland or Northern Ireland.)

Service Out of the Jurisdiction Where Permission of the Court Is Not Required

2.1 Where r. 6.34 applies, the claimant must file form N510 when filing the claim form.

Service Out of the Jurisdiction Where Permission Is Required

3.1 The claimant may serve a claim form out of the jurisdiction with the permission of the court under r. 6.36 where:

General grounds
(1) A claim is made for a remedy against a person domiciled within the jurisdiction.
(2) A claim is made for an injunction[(GL)] ordering the defendant to do or refrain from doing an act within the jurisdiction.
(3) A claim is made against a person ('the defendant') on whom the claim form has been or will be served (otherwise than in reliance on this paragraph) and:
   (a) there is between the claimant and the defendant a real issue which it is reasonable for the court to try; and
   (b) the claimant wishes to serve the claim form on another person who is a necessary or proper party to that claim.
(4) A claim is an additional claim under Part 20 and the person to be served is a necessary or proper party to the claim or additional claim.

Claims for interim remedies
(5) A claim is made for an interim remedy under section 25(1) of the Civil Jurisdiction and Judgments Act 1982.

Claims in relation to contracts
(6) A claim is made in respect of a contract where the contract:
   (a) was made within the jurisdiction;
   (b) was made by or through an agent trading or residing within the jurisdiction;
   (c) is governed by English law; or

(d) contains a term to the effect that the court shall have jurisdiction to determine any claim in respect of the contract.

(7) A claim is made in respect of a breach of contract committed within the jurisdiction.

(8) A claim is made for a declaration that no contract exists where, if the contract was found to exist, it would comply with the conditions set out in sub-para. (6).

Claims in tort

(9) A claim is made in tort where:
  (a) damage was sustained within the jurisdiction; or
  (b) the damage sustained resulted from an act committed within the jurisdiction.

Enforcement

(10) A claim is made to enforce any judgment or arbitral award.

Claims about property within the jurisdiction

(11) The whole subject matter of a claim relates to property located within the jurisdiction.

Claims about trusts etc.

(12) A claim is made for any remedy which might be obtained in proceedings to execute the trusts of a written instrument where:
  (a) the trusts ought to be executed according to English law; and
  (b) the person on whom the claim form is to be served is a trustee of the trusts.

(13) A claim is made for any remedy which might be obtained in proceedings for the administration of the estate of a person who died domiciled within the jurisdiction.

(14) A probate claim or a claim for the rectification of a will.

(15) A claim is made for a remedy against the defendant as constructive trustee where the defendant's alleged liability arises out of acts committed within the jurisdiction.

(16) A claim is made for restitution where the defendant's alleged liability arises out of acts committed within the jurisdiction.

Claims by HM Revenue and Customs

(17) A claim is made by the Commissioners for HM Revenue and Customs relating to duties or taxes against a defendant not domiciled in Scotland or Northern Ireland.

Claim for costs order in favour of or against third parties

(18) A claim is made by a party to proceedings for an order that the court exercise its power under the Supreme Court Act 1981, s. 51, to make a costs order in favour of or against a person who is not a party to those proceedings.

(Rule 48.2 sets out the procedure where the court is considering whether to exercise its discretion to make a costs order in favour of or against a non-party.)

Admiralty claims

(19) A claim is:
  (a) in the nature of salvage and any part of the services took place within the jurisdiction; or
  (b) to enforce a claim under the Merchant Shipping Act 1995, s. 153, 154,175 or 176A.

Claims under various enactments

(20) A claim is made:
  (a) under an enactment which allows proceedings to be brought and those proceedings are not covered by any of the other grounds referred to in this paragraph; or
  (b) under the Directive of the Council of the European Communities dated 15 March 1976 No. 76/308/EEC, where service is to be effected in a member State of the European Union.

Documents to Be Filed under r. 6.43(2)(c)

4.1 The claimant must provide the following documents for each party to be served out of the jurisdiction:

(1) a copy of the particulars of claim if not already contained in or served with the claim form;

(2) a duplicate of the claim form, of the particulars of claim (if not already contained in or served with the claim form) and of any documents accompanying the claim form;

(3) forms for responding to the claim; and

(4) any translation required under r. 6.45 in duplicate.

4.2 Some countries require legalisation of the document to be served and some require a formal letter of request which must be signed by the Senior Master. Any queries on this should be addressed to the Foreign Process Section (Room E02) at the Royal Courts of Justice.

Service in a Commonwealth State or British Overseas Territory

5.1 The judicial authorities of certain Commonwealth States which are not a party to the Hague Convention require service to be in accordance with r. 6.42(1)(b)(i) and not r. 6.42(3). A list of such countries can be obtained from the Foreign Process Section (Room E02) at the Royal Courts of Justice.

5.2 The list of British overseas territories is contained in the British Nationality Act 1981, sch. 6. For ease of reference, these are:
(a) Anguilla;
(b) Bermuda;
(c) British Antarctic Territory;
(d) British Indian Ocean Territory;
(e) British Virgin Islands;
(f) Cayman Islands;
(g) Falkland Islands;
(h) Gibraltar;
(i) Montserrat;
(j) Pitcairn, Henderson, Ducie and Oeno;
(k) St Helena and Dependencies;
(l) South Georgia and the South Sandwich Islands;
(m) Sovereign Base Areas of Akrotiri and Dhekelia; and
(n) Turks and Caicos Islands.

Period for Responding to a Claim Form

6.1 Where r. 6.35(5) applies, the periods within which the defendant must:
(1) file an acknowledgment of service;
(2) file or serve an admission; or
(3) file a defence,
will be calculated in accordance with para. 6.3, 6.4 or 6.5.

6.2 Where the court grants permission to serve a claim form out of the jurisdiction the court will determine in accordance with para. 6.3, 6.4 or 6.5 the periods within which the defendant must:
(1) file an acknowledgment of service;
(2) file or serve an admission; or
(3) file a defence.
(Rule 6.37(5)(a) provides that when giving permission to serve a claim form out of the jurisdiction the court will specify the period within which the defendant may respond to the claim form.)

6.3 The period for filing an acknowledgment of service under Part 10 or for filing or serving an admission under Part 14 is the number of days listed in the Table after service of the particulars of claim.

6.4 The period for filing a defence under Part 15 is:
(1) the number of days listed in the Table after service of the particulars of claim; or
(2) where the defendant has filed an acknowledgment of service, the number of days listed in the Table plus an additional 14 days after the service of the particulars of claim.

6.5 Under the State Immunity Act 1978, where a State is served, the period permitted under paras 6.3 and 6.4 for filing an acknowledgment of service or defence or for filing or serving an admission does not begin to run until two months after the date on which the State is served.

6.6 Where particulars of claim are served out of the jurisdiction any statement as to the period for responding to the claim contained in any of the forms required by r. 7.8 to accompany the particulars of claim must specify the period prescribed under r. 6.35 or by the order permitting service out of the jurisdiction under r. 6.37(5).

Period for Responding to an Application Notice

7.1 Where an application notice or order is served out of the jurisdiction, the period for responding is seven days less than the number of days listed in the Table.

Further information

7.2 Further information concerning service out of the jurisdiction can be obtained from the Foreign Process Section, Room E02, Royal Courts of Justice, Strand, London WC2A 2LL (telephone (020) 7947 6691).

Table

Place or country	Number of days	Place or country	Number of days
Afghanistan	23	Chad	25
Albania	25	Chile	22
Algeria	22	China	24
Andorra	21	China (Hong Kong)	31
Angola	22	China (Macau)	31
Anguilla	31	China (Taiwan)	23
Antigua and Barbuda	23	China (Tibet)	34
Antilles (Netherlands)	31	Christmas Island	27
Argentina	22	Cocos (Keeling) Islands	41
Armenia	21	Colombia	22
Ascension Island	31	Comoros	23
Australia	25	Congo (formerly Congo	
Austria	21	Brazzaville or French Congo)	25
Azerbaijan	22	Congo (Democratic Republic)	25
Azores	23	Corsica	21
Bahamas	22	Costa Rica	23
Bahrain	22	Croatia	21
Balearic Islands	21	Cuba	24
Bangladesh	23	Cyprus	31
Barbados	23	Czech Republic	21
Belarus	21	Denmark	21
Belgium	21	Djibouti	22
Belize	23	Dominica	23
Benin	25	Dominican Republic	23
Bermuda	31	East Timor	25
Bhutan	28	Ecuador	22
Bolivia	23	Egypt	22
Bosnia and Herzegovina	21	El Salvador	25
Botswana	23	Equatorial Guinea	23
Brazil	22	Eritrea	22
British Virgin Islands	31	Estonia	21
Brunei	25	Ethiopia	22
Bulgaria	23	Falkland Islands and Dependencies	31
Burkina Faso	23	Faroe Islands	31
Burma	23	Fiji	23
Burundi	22	Finland	24
Cambodia	28	France	21
Cameroon	22	French Guyana	31
Canada	22	French Polynesia	31
Canary Islands	22	French West Indies	31
Cape Verde	25	Gabon	25
Caroline Islands	31	Gambia	22
Cayman Islands	31	Georgia	21
Central African Republic	25	Germany	21

Place or country	Number of days	Place or country	Number of days
Ghana	22	Malta	21
Gibraltar	31	Mariana Islands	26
Greece	21	Marshall Islands	32
Greenland	31	Mauritania	23
Grenada	24	Mauritius	22
Guatemala	24	Mexico	23
Guernsey	21	Micronesia	23
Guinea	22	Moldova	21
Guinea-Bissau	22	Monaco	21
Guyana	22	Mongolia	24
Haiti	23	Montenegro	21
Holland (Netherlands)	21	Montserrat	31
Honduras	24	Morocco	22
Hungary	22	Mozambique	23
Iceland	22	Namibia	23
India	23	Nauru	36
Indonesia	22	Nepal	23
Iran	22	Netherlands	21
Iraq	22	Nevis	24
Ireland (Republic of)	21	New Caledonia	31
Ireland (Northern)	21	New Zealand	26
Isle of Man	21	New Zealand Island Territories	50
Israel	22	Nicaragua	24
Italy	21	Niger (Republic of)	25
Ivory Coast	22	Nigeria	22
Jamaica	22	Norfolk Island	31
Japan	23	Norway	21
Jersey	21	Oman (Sultanate of)	22
Jordan	23	Pakistan	23
Kazakhstan	21	Palau	23
Kenya	22	Panama	26
Kiribati	23	Papua New Guinea	26
Korea (North)	28	Paraguay	22
Korea (South)	24	Peru	22
Kosovo	21	Philippines	23
Kuwait	22	Pitcairn, Henderson, Ducie and	
Kyrgyzstan	21	Oeno Islands	31
Laos	30	Poland	21
Latvia	21	Portugal	21
Lebanon	22	Portuguese Timor*	31
Lesotho	23	Puerto Rico	23
Liberia	22	Qatar	23
Libya	21	Reunion	31
Liechtenstein	21	Romania	22
Lithuania	21	Russia	21
Luxembourg	21	Rwanda	23
Macedonia	21	Sabah	23
Madagascar	23	St Helena	31
Madeira	31	St Kitts and Nevis	24
Malawi	23	St Lucia	24
Malaysia	24		
Maldives	26		
Mali	25		

[* Now East Timor, for which there is a separate entry in the Table.]

Place or country	Number of days	Place or country	Number of days
St Pierre and Miquelon	31	Tajikistan	21
St Vincent and the Grenadines	24	Tanzania	22
Samoa (USA Territory) (See also		Thailand	23
Western Samoa)	30	Togo	22
San Marino	21	Tonga	30
Sao Tome and Principe	25	Trinidad and Tobago	23
Sarawak	28	Tristan da Cunha	31
Saudi Arabia	24	Tunisia	22
Scotland	21	Turkey	21
Senegal	22	Turkmenistan	21
Serbia	21	Turks & Caicos Islands	31
Seychelles	22	Tuvalu	23
Sierra Leone	22	Uganda	22
Singapore	22	Ukraine	21
Slovakia	21	United Arab Emirates	22
Slovenia	21	United States of America	22
Society Islands (French Polynesia)	31	Uruguay	22
Solomon Islands	29	Uzbekistan	21
Somalia	22	Vanuatu	29
South Africa	22	Vatican City State	21
South Georgia (Falkland Island		Venezuela	22
Dependencies)	31	Vietnam	28
South Orkneys	21	Virgin Islands — USA	24
South Shetlands	21	Wake Island	25
Spain	21	Western Samoa	34
Spanish Territories of North Africa	31	Yemen (Republic of)	30
Sri Lanka	23	Zaire*	25
Sudan	22	Zambia	23
Surinam	22	Zimbabwe	22
Swaziland	22		
Sweden	21		
Switzerland	21	[* Now Democratic Republic of the Congo, for which there is a separate entry in the Table.]	
Syria	23		

ANNEX

SERVICE REGULATION (r. 6.41)

[The text of Regulation (EC) No. 1393/2007 (the Service Regulation) may be downloaded from the Eurlex site: <http://eur-lex.europa.eu>]

CPR Part 7   How to Start Proceedings — The Claim Form

Amendment (a) effective from: 12 December 2008 insofar as it relates to European orders for payment under Regulation (EC) No. 1896/2006; 1 January 2009 insofar as it relates to the European small claims procedure under Regulation (EC) No. 861/2007. Amendments (b), (c) and (d) effective from: 1 October 2008. Source: SI 2008/2178, r. 6.

(a)   in rule 7.2, after the fourth parenthesis below paragraph (2) insert—
       '(Part 78 provides procedures for European orders for payment and for the European small claims procedure.)';

(b) in rule 7.4(3)—
    (i)   for 'he' substitute 'the claimant'; and
    (ii) omit 'together with a certificate of service';
(c) omit the parenthesis '(Rule 6.10 makes provision for a certificate of service).' below rule 7.4(3); and
(d) for rules 7.5 and 7.6 substitute—
    '7.5 Service of a claim form
    (1) Where the claim form is served within the jurisdiction, the claimant must complete the step required by the following table in relation to the particular method of service chosen, before 12.00 midnight on the calendar day four months after the date of issue of the claim form.

Method of service	Step required
First class post, document exchange or other service which provides for delivery on the next business day	Posting, leaving with, delivering to or collection by the relevant service provider
Delivery of the document to or leaving it at the relevant place	Delivering to or leaving the document at the relevant place
Personal service under rule 6.5	Completing the relevant step required by rule 6.5(3)
Fax	Completing the transmission of the fax
Other electronic method	Sending the e-mail or other electronic transmission

(2) Where the claim form is to be served out of the jurisdiction, the claim form must be served in accordance with Section IV of Part 6 within 6 months of the date of issue.

7.6 Extension of time for serving a claim form

(1) The claimant may apply for an order extending the period for compliance with rule 7.5.
(2) The general rule is that an application to extend the time for compliance with rule 7.5 must be made—
    (a) within the period specified by rule 7.5; or
    (b) where an order has been made under this rule, within the period for service specified by that order.
(3) If the claimant applies for an order to extend the time for compliance after the end of the period specified by rule 7.5 or by an order made under this rule, the court may make such an order only if—
    (a) the court has failed to serve the claim form; or
    (b) the claimant has taken all reasonable steps to comply with rule 7.5 but has been unable to do so; and
    (c) in either case, the claimant has acted promptly in making the application.
(4) An application for an order extending the time for compliance with rule 7.5—
    (a) must be supported by evidence; and
    (b) may be made without notice.'.

PD 7   Practice Direction — How to Start Proceedings — The Claim Form

Amendment effective from: 1 October 2008. Source: 47th Update.

(1) For para. 3.5 substitute:
    '3.5 Where a claim form to be served out of the jurisdiction is one which the court has power to deal with:
    (a) under the Civil Jurisdiction and Judgments Act 1982; and
    (b) the Judgments Regulation (which has the same meaning as in r. 6.31(d)),

the claim form must, pursuant to r. 6.34, be filed and served with the notice referred to in that rule and PD 6B, para. 2.1.'.
(2) Omit para. 3.5A.
(3) In para. 6.1(2):
    (a) for the footnote to 'claim form' substitute the footnote 'See rules 7.4(2) and 7.5(1).'; and
    (b) for the footnote to 'jurisdiction' substitute the footnote 'See rule 7.5(2).'.

PD 7B   Practice Direction — Consumer Credit Act Claim

Amendment effective from: 1 October 2008. Source: 47th Update.

(1) In para. 4.3, after 'section 129(1)(b)' insert 'or 129(1)(ba)'.
(2) In para. 7.3:
    (a) after 'section 129(1)(b)' insert 'or 129(1)(ba)'; and
    (b) for 'his particulars' substitute 'the particulars'.
(3) After para. 7.3 insert:
    '7.3A A claimant who is a debtor or hirer making a claim for an order under s. 129(1)(ba) of the Act must attach to the particulars of claim a copy of the notice served on the creditor or owner under s. 129A(1)(a) of the Act.'.

PD 7C   Practice Direction — Production Centre

Amendment effective from: 1 October 2008. Source: 47th Update.

In para. 1.4(3):
(a) for 'Rule 6.3(3)' substitute 'Rules 6.4(3) and 6.21(4)'; and
(b) for 'does' substitute 'do'.

CPR Part 8   Alternative Procedure for Claims

Amendment effective from: 12 December 2008 insofar as it relates to European orders for payment under Regulation (EC) No. 1896/2006; 1 January 2009 insofar as it relates to the European small claims procedure under Regulation (EC) No. 861/2007. Source: SI 2008/2178, r. 7.

In rule 8.1, after the parenthesis below paragraph (6) insert—

'(Part 78 provides procedures for European orders for payment and for the European small claims procedure.)'.

PD 8   Practice Direction — Alternative Procedure for Claims

Amendment effective from: 1 October 2008. Source: 47th Update.

In the parenthesis below para. 20.5, after 'method' insert 'or at an alternative place'.

CPR Part 10   Acknowledgment of Service

Amendment effective from: 1 October 2008. Source: SI 2008/2178, r. 8.

(a) in rule 10.3(2)—
  (i)   in sub-paragraph (a)—
      (aa) for '6.22' substitute '6.35'; and
      (bb) after 'jurisdiction' insert 'under rule 6.32 or 6.33';
  (ii) in sub-paragraph (b), for '6.16(4)' substitute '6.12(3)'; and
  (iii) in sub-paragraph (c)—
      (aa) for '6.21(4)' substitute '6.37(5)'; and
      (bb) for 'Practice Direction 6B' substitute 'Practice Direction B supplementing Part 6';
(b) in rule 10.5(a) for 'his' substitute 'the defendant's'; and
(c) in the first parenthesis below rule 10.5(b)—
  (i)   for '6.5' substitute '6.23'; and
  (ii) for 'jurisdiction' substitute 'United Kingdom'.

PD 10   Practice Direction — Acknowledgment of Service

Amendment effective from: 1 October 2008. Source: 47th Update.

(1) In para. 3.1:
  (a) for 'his' substitute 'the'; and
  (b) for the footnote to 'documents' substitute the footnote 'See r. 6.23'.
(2) In para. 3.2, for 'rule 6.5 and the practice direction which supplements Part 6' substitute 'r. 6.23'.
(3) For the parenthesis below para. 5.5 substitute:
    '(PD 6A, para. 8.2, contains provisions about service by the court on the claimant of any notice of funding filed with an acknowledgment of service.)'.

CPR Part 12   Default Judgment

Amendment effective from: 1 October 2008. Source: SI 2008/2178, r. 9.

(a) for the second parenthesis below rule 12.3(3)(c)(ii) substitute—
    '(Rule 6.17 provides that, where the claim form is served by the claimant, the claimant may not obtain default judgment unless a certificate of service has been filed.)';
(b) for the third parenthesis below rule 12.3(3)(c)(ii) substitute—
    '(Article 19(1) of the Service Regulation (which has the same meaning as in rule 6.31(e)) applies in relation to judgment in default where the claim form is served in accordance with that Regulation.)';
(c) in rule 12.4(4), for 'rule 6.5(8)' substitute 'rule 6.10';
(d) in rule 12.10—
  (i)   at the beginning of paragraph (b) for 'he' substitute 'the claimant';
  (ii) in paragraph (b)(i)—
      (aa) for '6.19(1) or (1A)' substitute '6.32(1), 6.33(1) or 6.33(2)'; and
      (bb) for 'service without leave' substitute 'service where permission of the court is not required'; and
  (iii) in paragraph (b)(ii), for 'Regulation State' substitute 'Member State';
(e) in rule 12.11(4)(a), for '6.19(1) or 6.19(1A)' substitute '6.32(1), 6.33(1) or 6.33(2)'; and

(f) in rule 12.11(6)—
  (i) in sub-paragraph (a)(ii), for 'Regulation State' substitute 'Member State';
  (ii) in sub-paragraph (d), after ';' insert 'and';
  (iii) in sub-paragraph (e), for '; and' substitute '.'; and
  (iv) omit sub-paragraph (f).

PD 12   Practice Direction — Default Judgment

Amendment effective from: 1 October 2008. Source: 47th Update.

In para. 4.3(2) for 'Regulation State' substitute 'member State'.

CPR Part 13   Setting Aside or Varying Default Judgment

Amendment effective from: 1 October 2008. Source: SI 2008/2178, r. 10.

For the second parenthesis below rule 13.3(2) substitute—

'(Article 19(4) of the Service Regulation (which has the same meaning as in rule 6.31(e)) applies to applications to appeal a judgment in default when the time limit for appealing has expired.)'.

CPR Part 14   Admissions

Amendment effective from: 1 October 2008. Source: SI 2008/2178, r. 11.

In rule 14.2(2)—
(a) in sub-paragraph (a)—
  (i) for '6.22' substitute '6.35'; and
  (ii) after 'jurisdiction' insert 'under rule 6.32 or 6.33'; and
(b) in sub-paragraph (b), for '6.16(4)' substitute '6.12(3)'.

CPR Part 15   Defence and Reply

Amendment effective from: 1 October 2008. Source: SI 2008/2178, r. 12.

In rule 15.4(2)—
(a) in sub-paragraph (a)—
  (i) for '6.23' substitute '6.35'; and
  (ii) after 'jurisdiction' insert 'under rule 6.32 or 6.33';
(b) in sub-paragraph (b), for 'he' substitute 'the defendant'; and
(c) in sub-paragraph (d), for '6.16(4)' substitute '6.12(3)'.

PD 15   Practice Direction — Defence and Reply

Amendment effective from: 1 October 2008. Source: 47th Update.

For the parenthesis below para. 3.4 substitute:

'(PD 6A, para. 8.2, contains provisions about service by the court on the claimant of any notice of funding filed with a defence.)'.

CPR Part 16   Statements of Case

Amendment effective from: 1 October 2008. Source: SI 2008/2178, r. 13.

(a) in rule 16.5(8), for 'he' substitute 'the defendant'; and
(b) in the second parenthesis below rule 16.5(8)—
    (i) for '6.5' substitute '6.23'; and
    (ii) for 'jurisdiction' substitute 'United Kingdom'.

PD 16   Practice Direction — Statements of Case

Amendment effective from: 1 October 2008. Source: 47th Update.

(1) Omit the first parenthesis below para. 2.6(e).
(2) In para. 3.2(2):
    (a) for the footnote to 'claim form' substitute the footnote 'See rr. 7.4(2) and 7.5(1).'; and
    (b) for the footnote to 'jurisdiction' substitute the footnote 'See r. 7.5(2).'.

PD 18   Practice Direction — Further Information

Amendment effective from: 1 October 2008. Source: 47th Update.

In para. 1.7:

(a) after 'the provisions of' insert 'r. 6.23(5) and (6) and'; and
(b) for 'PD 6, paras 3.1 to 3.3' substitute 'PD 6A, paras 4.1 to 4.3'.

CPR Part 20   Counterclaims and Other Additional Claims

Amendment effective from: 1 October 2008. Source: SI 2008/2178, r. 14.

For the parenthesis below rule 20.13(2) substitute—

'(Part 66 contains provisions about counterclaims and other Part 20 claims in relation to proceedings by or against the Crown.)'.

CPR Part 21   Children and Protected Parties

Amendment effective from: 1 October 2008. Source: SI 2008/2178, r. 15.

(a) in the first parenthesis below rule 21.1(2)(e), for 'Rule 6.6 contains' substitute 'Rules 6.13 and 6.25 contain';
(b) in rule 21.5(4)—
    (i)   in sub-paragraph (a), for '6.6' substitute '6.13'; and
    (ii) in sub-paragraph (b), for 'he files' substitute 'filing';
(c) in the parenthesis below rule 21.5(4)(b), for 'Rule 6.10 sets' substitute 'Rules 6.17 and 6.29 set'; and
(d) in rule 21.8(1), for '6.6' substitute '6.13'.

PD 22   Practice Direction — Statements of Truth

Amendment effective from: 1 October 2008. Source: 47th Update.

In para. 3.4:
(a) for the footnote to 'senior position' substitute the footnote 'PD 6A, para. 6.2, sets out the meaning of 'senior position'.'; and
(b) for 'he holds' substitute 'held'.

PD 25B   Practice Direction — Interim Payments

Amendment effective from: 1 October 2008. Source: 47th Update.

(1) For para. 4.1 substitute:
    '4.1 Where in a claim for personal injuries there is an application for an interim payment of damages:
(1) which is other than by consent;
(2) which either:
    (i)   falls under the heads of damage set out in the Social Security (Recovery of Benefits) Act 1997 ('the 1997 Act'), sch. 2, col. 1, in respect of recoverable benefits received by the claimant set out in col. 2 of that schedule; or
    (ii) includes damages in respect of a disease for which a lump sum payment within the definition in s. 1A(2) of the 1997 Act has been, or is likely to be made; and
(3) where the defendant is liable to pay a recoverable amount (as defined in r. 36.15(1)(c)) to the Secretary of State,
the defendant should obtain from the Secretary of State a certificate (as defined in r. 36.15(1)(e)).'.
(2) In para. 4.2, for 'should' substitute 'must'.
(3) For para. 4.3 substitute:
    '4.3 The order will set out the deductible amount (as defined in r. 36.15(1)(d)).'.

CPR Part 26   Case Management — Preliminary Stage

Amendment effective from: 1 October 2008. Source: SI 2008/2178, r. 16.

In the second parenthesis below rule 26.3(7), for 'Rule 6.7 specifies' substitute 'Rules 6.14 and 6.26 specify'.

CPR Part 36   Offers to Settle

Amendment effective from: 1 October 2008. Source: SI 2008/2178, r. 17.

(a) in the table of contents, for 'Deduction of benefits' substitute 'Deduction of benefits and lump sum payments';

(b) in rule 36.9—

    (i) in paragraph 3(b), for 'benefits' substitute 'amounts'; and

    (ii) for the second parenthesis below paragraph (3)(d) substitute—

        '(Rule 36.15 defines 'deductible amounts'.)';

(c) in rule 36.10—

    (i) in paragraph (1), for 'his' substitute 'the';

    (ii) in paragraph (2), for 'his' substitute 'the';

    (iii) below the parenthesis following paragraph (3), insert—

        '(Rule 44.12 contains provisions about when a costs order is deemed to have been made and applying for an order under section 194(3) of the Legal Services Act 2007.)'; and

    (iv) in paragraph (5)(a), for 'his' substitute 'the'; and

(d) in rule 36.15—

    (i) for the heading to rule 36.15 and for paragraphs (1) and (2) substitute—

    '36.15 Deduction of benefits and lump sum payments

      (1) In this rule and rule 36.9—

        (a) 'the 1997 Act' means the Social Security (Recovery of Benefits) Act 1997;

        (b) 'the 2008 Regulations' means the Social Security (Recovery of Benefits) (Lump Sum Payments) Regulations 2008;

        (c) 'recoverable amount' means—

            (i) 'recoverable benefits' as defined in section 1(4)(c) of the 1997 Act; and

            (ii) 'recoverable lump sum payments' as defined in regulation 4 of the 2008 Regulations;

        (d) 'deductible amount' means—

            (i) any benefits by the amount of which damages are to be reduced in accordance with section 8 of, and Schedule 2 to the 1997 Act ('deductible benefits'); and

            (ii) any lump sum payment by the amount of which damages are to be reduced in accordance with regulation 12 of the 2008 Regulations ('deductible lump sum payments'); and

        (e) 'certificate'—

            (i) in relation to recoverable benefits is construed in accordance with the provisions of the 1997 Act; and

            (ii) in relation to recoverable lump sum payments has the meaning given in section 29 of the 1997 Act as applied by regulation 2 of, and modified by Schedule 1 to the 2008 Regulations.

      (2) This rule applies where a payment to a claimant following acceptance of a Part 36 offer would be a compensation payment as defined in section 1(4)(b) or 1A(5)(b) of the 1997 Act.';

    (ii) in paragraph (3)—

      (aa) in sub-paragraph (a), for 'benefits' substitute 'amounts'; and

      (bb) in sub-paragraph (b) for 'benefits' substitute 'amounts';

    (iii) in paragraph (5), omit 'of recoverable benefits';

    (iv) in paragraph (6)(b)—

      (aa) for 'benefit' substitute 'amount'; and

      (bb) for 'that' substitute 'the';

    (v) in paragraph (6)(c), for 'after deduction of the amount of benefit' substitute 'of compensation';

    (vi) for paragraph (7) substitute—

        '(7) If at the time the offeror makes the Part 36 offer, the offeror has applied for, but has not received a certificate, the offeror must clarify the offer by stating the matters referred to in paragraphs (6)(b) and (6)(c) not more than 7 days after receipt of the certificate.';

    (vii) in paragraph (8)—

(aa) for 'he' substitute 'the claimant'; and
(bb) for 'benefits' substitute 'amounts';
(viii) for the parenthesis following paragraph (8) substitute—
'(Section 15(2) of the 1997 Act provides that the court must specify the compensation payment attributable to each head of damage. Schedule 1 to the 2008 Regulations modifies section 15 of the 1997 Act in relation to lump sum payments and provides that the court must specify the compensation payment attributable to each or any dependant who has received a lump sum payment.)'; and
(ix) in paragraph (9) and in the parenthesis following paragraph (9), in each place where it appears, for 'benefits' substitute 'amounts'.

PD 36   Practice Direction — Offers to Settle

Amendment effective from: 1 October 2008. Source: 47th Update.

(1) In para. 3.3(1):
(a) in sub-para. (b), for 'benefits' substitute 'amounts'; and
(b) in sub-para. (c), for 'benefits' substitute 'amounts'.
(2) In para. 3.3(2), omit 'of recoverable benefits'.

CPR Part 38   Discontinuance

Amendment effective from: 1 October 2008. Source: SI 2008/2178, rr. 18 and 19.

In rule 38.6—
(a) in paragraph (1)—
(i)   for 'he' substitute 'the claimant'; and
(ii)   for 'him' substitute 'the defendant'; and
(b) in the parenthesis below paragraph (3)—
(i)   after 'where' insert 'the'; and
(ii)   after 'discontinuance' insert 'and contains provisions about when a costs order is deemed to have been made and applying for an order under section 194(3) of the Legal Services Act 2007'.
In rule 38.8—
(a) for paragraph (1)(b) substitute—
'(b) a claimant is liable to—
(i)   pay costs under rule 38.6; or
(ii)   make a payment pursuant to an order under section 194(3) of the Legal Services Act 2007; and';
(b) in paragraph (1)(c)—
(i)   after 'those costs' insert 'or make the payment'; and
(ii)   in sub-paragraph (ii) after 'to be paid' insert 'or the payment to be made';
(c) in paragraph (2)—
(i)   for 'he' substitute 'the claimant'; and
(ii)   after 'rule 38.6' insert 'or makes the payment pursuant to an order under section 194(3) of the Legal Services Act 2007'; and
(d) below paragraph (2) insert—
'(Rules 44.3C and 44.12 contain provisions about applying for an order under section 194(3) of the Legal Services Act 2007.)'.

CPR Part 40   Judgments, Orders, Sale of Land etc.

Amendment effective from: 1 October 2008. Source: SI 2008/2178, r. 20.

For the parenthesis below rule 40.4(2)(b) substitute—

'(Rule 6.21 sets out who is to serve a document other than the claim form.)'.

PD 40B   Practice Direction — Judgments and Orders

Amendment effective from: 1 October 2008. Source: 47th Update.

(1) For para. 5.1 substitute:

'5.1 In a final judgment where some or all of the damages awarded:
(1) fall under the heads of damage set out in the Social Security (Recovery of Benefits) Act 1997 ('the 1997 Act'), sch. 2, col. 1, in respect of recoverable benefits received by the claimant set out in col. 2 of that schedule; and
(2) where the defendant has paid to the Secretary of State the recoverable benefits in accordance with the certificate (as defined in r. 36.15(1)(e)),

there will be stated in the preamble to the judgment or order the amount awarded under each head of damage and the amount by which it has been reduced in accordance with s. 8 of and sch. 2 to the 1997 Act.'.

(2) After para. 5.1 insert:

'5.1A Where damages are awarded in a case where a lump sum payment (to be construed in accordance with s. 1A of the 1997 Act) has been made to a dependant, then s. 15 of the 1997 Act (as modified by the Social Security (Recovery of Benefits) (Lump Sum Payments) Regulations 2008 (SI 2008/1596), sch. 1) sets out what the court order must contain.'.

PD 40E   Practice Direction — Reserved Judgments

Amendment effective from: 1 October 2008. Source: 47th Update.

PD 40E is replaced by the following new PD 40E.

PD 40E   Practice Direction — Reserved Judgments

This practice direction supplements CPR, Part 40.

Scope and Interpretation

1.1 This practice direction applies to all reserved judgments which the court intends to hand down in writing.

1.2 In this practice direction:
(a) 'relevant court office' means the office of the court in which judgment is to be given; and
(b) 'working day' means any day on which the relevant court office is open.

Availability of Reserved Judgments before Handing Down

2.1 Where judgment is to be reserved the judge (or presiding judge) may, at the conclusion of the hearing, invite the views of the parties' legal representatives as to the arrangements made for the handing down of the judgment.

2.2 Unless the court directs otherwise, the following provisions of this paragraph apply where the judge or presiding judge is satisfied that the judgment will attract no special degree of confidentiality or sensitivity.

2.3 The court will provide a copy of the draft judgment to the parties' legal representatives by 4 p.m. on the second working day before handing down, or at such other time as the court may direct.

2.4 A copy of the draft judgment may be supplied, in confidence, to the parties provided that:
(a) neither the draft judgment nor its substance is disclosed to any other person or used in the public domain; and
(b) no action is taken (other than internally) in response to the draft judgment, before the judgment is handed down.

2.5 Where a copy of the draft judgment is supplied to a party's legal representatives in electronic form, they may supply a copy to that party in the same form.

2.6 If a party to whom a copy of the draft judgment is supplied under para. 2.4 is a partnership, company, government department, local authority or other organisation of a similar nature, additional copies may be distributed in confidence within the organisation, provided that all reasonable steps are taken to preserve its confidential nature and the requirements of para. 2.4 are adhered to.

2.7 If the parties or their legal representatives are in any doubt about the persons to whom copies of the draft judgment may be distributed they should enquire of the judge or presiding judge.

2.8 Any breach of the obligations or restrictions under para. 2.4 or failure to take all reasonable steps under para. 2.6 may be treated as contempt of court.

2.9 The case will be listed for judgment, and judgment handed down at the appropriate time.

Corrections to the Draft Judgment

3.1 Unless the parties or their legal representatives are told otherwise when the draft judgment is circulated, any proposed corrections to the draft judgment should be sent to the clerk of the judge who prepared the draft with a copy to any other party.

Orders Consequential on Judgment

4.1 Following the circulation of the draft judgment the parties or their legal representatives must seek to agree orders consequential upon the judgment.

4.2 In respect of any draft agreed order the parties must:
(a) fax or email a copy to the clerk to the judge or presiding judge (together with any proposed corrections or amendments to the draft judgment); and
(b) file four copies (with completed backsheets) in the relevant court office, by 12 noon on the working day before handing down.

4.3 A copy of a draft order must bear the case reference, the date of handing down and the name of the judge or presiding judge.

4.4 Where a party wishes to apply for an order consequential on the judgment the application must be made by filing written submissions with the clerk to the judge or presiding judge by 12 noon on the working day before handing down.

4.5 Unless the court orders otherwise:
(a) where judgment is to be given by an appeal court (which has the same meaning as in r. 52.1(3)(b)), the application will be determined without a hearing; and
(b) where judgment is to be given by any other court, the application will be determined at a hearing.

Attendance at Handing Down

5.1 If there is not to be an oral hearing of an application for an order consequential on judgment:

(a) the parties' advocates need not attend on the handing down of judgment; and

(b) the judgment may be handed down by a judge sitting alone.

5.2 Where para. 5.1(a) applies but an advocate does attend the handing down of judgment, the court may if it considers such attendance unnecessary, disallow the costs of the attendance.

CPR Part 42   Change of Solicitor

Amendment effective from: 1 October 2008. Source: SI 2008/2178, r. 21.

For the first parenthesis below rule 42.2(6)(b)(ii) substitute—

'(Rules 6.23 and 6.24 contain provisions about a party's address for service.)'.

PD 42   Practice Direction — Change of Solicitor

Amendment effective from: 1 October 2008. Source: 47th Update.

(1) In para. 1.1:

(a) for the footnote to 'business address' substitute the footnote 'Rules 6.7 and 6.23 contain provisions about service on the business address of a solicitor.'; and

(b) for 'his' substitute 'that party's'.

(2) In para. 2.4:

(a) for 'his' substitute 'the'; and

(b) for 'jurisdiction.⁵' substitute 'United Kingdom.⁵' (with new footnote, '⁵ See r. 6.23.').

(3) In para. 5.1, for 'with r. 6.5(2)' substitute 'with rr. 6.23(1) and 6.24'.

(4) For the first parenthesis below para. 5.1 substitute:

'(Rule 6.23 provides that a party must give an address for service within the United Kingdom.)'.

(5) In the second parenthesis below para. 5.1, for '6.5(6)' substitute '6.9'.

CPR Part 43   Scope of Cost Rules and Definitions

Amendment effective from: 1 October 2008. Source: SI 2008/2178, r. 22.

In rule 43.2(1)—

(a) in sub-paragraph (e), for 'his' substitute 'that';

(b) in sub-paragraph (k)(iii), for 'his' substitute 'that person's';

(c) in sub-paragraph (n) omit 'and';

(d) in sub-paragraph (o) for '.' substitute ';'; and

(e) after sub-paragraph (o) insert—

'(p) 'free of charge' has the same meaning as in section 194(10) of the Legal Services Act 2007;

(q) 'pro bono representation' means legal representation provided free of charge; and

(r) 'the prescribed charity' has the same meaning as in section 194(8) of the Legal Services Act 2007.'.

CPR Part 44   General Rules about Costs

Amendment effective from: 1 October 2008. Source: SI 2008/2178, r. 23.

In Part 44—

(a) in the table of contents, after the entry 'Limits on recovery under funding arrangements' insert the entry—
'Orders in respect of pro bono representation Rule 44.3C';

(b) in rule 44.1, for 'costs and entitlement to costs' substitute 'costs, entitlement to costs and orders in respect of pro bono representation';

(c) after rule 44.3B insert—

'44.3C Orders in respect of pro bono representation

(1) In this rule, 'the 2007 Act' means the Legal Services Act 2007.

(2) Where the court makes an order under section 194(3) of the 2007 Act—

    (a) the court may order the payment to the prescribed charity of a sum no greater than the costs specified in Part 45 to which the party with pro bono representation would have been entitled in accordance with that Part and in respect of that representation had it not been provided free of charge; or

    (b) where Part 45 does not apply, the court may determine the amount of the payment (other than a sum equivalent to fixed costs) to be made by the paying party to the prescribed charity by—

        (i) making a summary assessment; or

        (ii) making an order for detailed assessment,

of a sum equivalent to all or part of the costs the paying party would have been ordered to pay to the party with pro bono representation in respect of that representation had it not been provided free of charge.

(3) Where the court makes an order under section 194(3) of the 2007 Act, the order must specify that the payment by the paying party must be made to the prescribed charity.

(4) The receiving party must send a copy of the order to the prescribed charity within 7 days of receipt of the order.

(5) Where the court considers making or makes an order under section 194(3) of the 2007 Act, Parts 43 to 48 apply, where appropriate, with the following modifications—

    (a) references to 'costs orders', 'orders about costs' or 'orders for the payment of costs' are to be read, unless otherwise stated, as if they refer to an order under section 194(3);

    (b) references to 'costs' are to be read, as if they referred to a sum equivalent to the costs that would have been claimed by, incurred by or awarded to the party with pro bono representation in respect of that representation had it not been provided free of charge; and

    (c) references to 'receiving party' are to be read, as meaning a party who has pro bono representation and who would have been entitled to be paid costs in respect of that representation had it not been provided free of charge.';

(d) in rule 44.12, after paragraph (1) insert—
'(1A) Where such an order is deemed to be made in favour of a party with pro bono representation, that party may apply for an order under section 194(3) of the Legal Services Act 2007.'; and

(e) in rule 44.13(1)—

    (i) for sub-paragraph (a) substitute—

'(a) subject to paragraphs (1A) and (1B), the general rule is that no party is entitled—

    (i) to costs; or

    (ii) to seek an order under section 194(3) of the Legal Services Act 2007, in relation to that order; but'; and

    (ii) in sub-paragraph (b) for 'him' substitute 'that party'.

CPR Part 45   Fixed Costs

Amendment effective from: 1 October 2008. Source: SI 2008/2178, r. 24.

In Table 4 below rule 45.5, for the entry—

'Where service by an alternative method is permitted by an order under rule 6.8 for each individual served £53.25' substitute—

'Where service by an alternative method or at an alternative place is permitted by an order under rule 6.15 for each individual served £53.25'.

CPR Part 47   Procedure for Detailed Assessment of Costs and Default Provisions

Amendment effective from: 1 October 2008. Source: SI 2008/2178, r. 25.

(a) for rule 47.5 substitute—

'**47.5 Application of this Section**

This Section of Part 47 applies where a cost officer is to make a detailed assessment of—

(a) costs which are payable by one party to another; or

(b) the sum which is payable by one party to the prescribed charity pursuant to an order under section 194(3) of the Legal Services Act 2007.';

(b) in rule 47.11—

  (i) in paragraph (1), for 'he' substitute 'that party';

  (ii) in paragraph (3)—

    (aa) for 'him' substitute 'that party'; and

    (bb) for 'shall' substitute 'will'; and

  (iii) after paragraph (3) insert—

    '(4) A receiving party who obtains a default costs certificate in detailed assessment proceedings pursuant to an order under section 194(3) of the Legal Services Act 2007 must send a copy of the default costs certificate to the prescribed charity.';

(c) in rule 47.12, after the parenthesis below paragraph (4) insert—

  '(5) Where the court sets aside or varies a default costs certificate in detailed assessment proceedings pursuant to an order under section 194(3) of the Legal Services Act 2007, the receiving party must send a copy of the order setting aside or varying the default costs certificate to the prescribed charity.';

(d) in rule 47.15, after paragraph (3) insert—

  '(4) Where the court—

    (a) issues an interim costs certificate; or

    (b) amends or cancels an interim certificate,

in detailed assessment proceedings pursuant to an order under section 194(3) of the Legal Services Act 2007, the receiving party must send a copy of the interim costs certificate or the order amending or cancelling the interim costs certificate to the prescribed charity.';

(e) in rule 47.16, after the parenthesis below paragraph (5) insert—

  '(6) Where the court issues a final costs certificate in detailed assessment proceedings pursuant to an order under section 194(3) of the Legal Services Act 2007, the receiving party must send a copy of the final costs certificate to the prescribed charity.'; and

(f) in rule 47.18—

  (i) in paragraph (1), for 'his' substitute 'the'; and

  (ii) after paragraph (1) insert—

    '(1A) Paragraph (1) does not apply where the receiving party has pro bono representation in the detailed assessment proceedings but that party may apply for an order in respect of that representation under section 194(3) of the Legal Services Act 2007.'.

PD 43–48   Practice Direction about Costs

Amendment effective from: 1 October 2008. Source: 47th Update.

(1) In para. 4.2:
   (a) for 'A division into parts will be necessary or convenient in the following circumstances' substitute 'Circumstances in which it will be necessary or convenient to divide a bill into parts include';
   (b) in sub-para. (1):
      (i) for 'he' substitute 'that party'; and
      (ii) for 'should' substitute 'must';
   (c) after para. (1) insert:
      '(1A) Where the receiving party had pro bono representation for part of the proceedings and an order under the Legal Services Act 2007, s. 194(3), has been made, the bill must be divided into different parts so as to distinguish between:
(a) the sum equivalent to the costs claimed for work done by the legal representative acting free of charge; and
(b) the costs claimed for work done by the legal representative not acting free of charge.'; and
   (d) in sub-paras (2), (3), (4), (5) and (6) each time it occurs, for 'should' substitute 'must'.
(2) After para. 5.20, insert:

'Payment Pursuant to an Order under the Legal Services Act 2007, s. 194(3)

5.21 Where an order is made under the Legal Services Act 2007, s. 194(3), any bill presented for agreement or assessment pursuant to that order must not include a claim for VAT.'.
(3) For para. 6.2 substitute:
   '6.2(1) In this Section an 'estimate of costs' means:
      (a) an estimate of costs of:
         (i) base costs (including disbursements) already incurred; and
         (ii) base costs (including disbursements) to be incurred,
      which a party, if successful in the proceedings, intends to seek to recover from any other party under an order for costs; or
      (b) in proceedings where the party has pro bono representation and intends, if successful in the proceedings, to seek an order under the Legal Services Act 2007, s. 194(3), an estimate of the sum equivalent to:
         (i) the base costs (including disbursements) that the party would have already incurred had the legal representation provided to that party not been free of charge; and
         (ii) the base costs (including disbursements) that the party would incur if the legal representation to be provided to that party were not free of charge.
   ('Base costs' are defined in para. 2.2 of this practice direction.)
   (2) A party who intends to recover an additional liability (defined in r. 43.2) need not reveal the amount of that liability in the estimate.'.
(4) After para. 10.2 insert:

'SECTION 10A ORDERS IN RESPECT OF PRO BONO REPRESENTATION: RULE 44.3C

10A.1 Rule 44.3C(2) sets out how the court may determine the amount of payment when making an order under the Legal Services Act 2007, s. 194(3). Paragraph 13.2 of this practice direction provides that the general rule is that the court will make a summary assessment of costs in the circumstances outlined in that paragraph unless there is good reason not to do so. This will apply to r. 44.3C(2)(b) with the modification that the summary assessment of the costs is to be read as meaning the summary assessment of the sum equivalent to the costs that would have been claimed by the party with pro bono representation in respect of that representation had it not been provided free of charge.

10A.2 Where an order under the Legal Services Act 2007, s. 194(3), is sought, to assist the court in making a summary assessment of the amount payable to the prescribed charity, the party who has pro bono representation must prepare, file and serve in accordance with para. 13.5(2) a written statement of the sum equivalent to the costs that party would have claimed for that legal representation had it not been provided free of charge.'.

(5) In para. 32.9(2), for 'Part 6, Section III' substitute 'Section IV of Part 6'.

(6) In para. 35.4(2), for 'Part 6, Section III' substitute 'Section IV of Part 6'.

PD 51B   Practice Direction — Automatic Orders Pilot Scheme

New PD 51B takes effect on 1 October 2008. Source: 47th Update.

This practice direction supplements CPR, Parts 26 and 28.

General

1.1 This practice direction is made under r. 51.2. It provides for a pilot scheme ('the Automatic Orders Pilot Scheme') to:

(1) operate from 1 October 2008 to 30 September 2009;

(2) operate in the county courts at Chelmsford, Newcastle, Teesside, Watford and York; and

(3) apply to claims started on or after 1 October 2008.

1.2 The Automatic Orders Pilot Scheme will apply to claims where:

(1) all parties request a stay of proceedings for one month;

(2) any party fails to file an allocation questionnaire; or

(3) in cases with only one claimant and one defendant and which are allocated to the fast track, a party fails to file a pre-trial checklist.

Amendments to Part 26 and Part 28

2 During the operation of the Automatic Orders Pilot Scheme:

Stay of proceedings for one month

(1) Rule 26.4 is modified by substituting for para. (2) the following:

'(2)

(a) Where all parties request a stay under para. (1), the proceedings will be stayed for one month and the court will notify the parties to that effect.

(b) Any request for a further stay will be considered under r. 26.4(3).

(c) Where the court, of its own initiative, considers that such a stay would be appropriate, the court will direct that the proceedings, either in whole or in part, be stayed for one month, or for such specified period as the court considers appropriate.'.

Failure by a party to file an allocation questionnaire

(2) PD 26 is modified by substituting for para. 2.5 the following:

'2.5

(1) Where a party does not file an allocation questionnaire within the time specified by form N152, the court will serve a notice on that party requiring the allocation questionnaire to be filed within seven days from service of the notice.

(2) Where a party does not file the allocation questionnaire within the period specified in the notice served pursuant to sub-para. (1) then that party's claim, defence or counterclaim (as appropriate) will automatically be struck out without further order of the court.'.

Failure to file a pre-trial checklist in a case allocated to the fast track

(3) Where there is only one claimant and one defendant and the case is allocated to the fast track then r. 28.5 is modified by substituting for sub-paras (3) and (4) the following:

'(3) Where a party does not file a pre-trial checklist the court will serve a notice on that party requiring the pre-trial checklist to be filed within seven days from service of the notice.

(4) Where that party does not file the pre-trial checklist within the period specified in the notice served pursuant to sub-para. (3) then that party's claim, defence or counterclaim (as appropriate) will automatically be struck out without further order of the court.

(5) If:
- (a) a party has failed to give all the information requested by the pre-trial checklist; or
- (b) the court considers that a hearing is necessary to enable it to decide what directions to give in order to complete preparation of the case for trial,

the court may give such directions as it thinks appropriate.'.

(4) Where there is only one claimant and one defendant and the case is allocated to the fast track then the PD 28 is modified by:
- (a) substituting for para. 6.1(3) the following:
  '(3) When all the pre-trial checklists have been filed the court file will be placed before a judge for directions.'; and
- (b) disapplying paras 6.4 and 6.5.

CPR Part 52   Appeals

Amendment effective from: 1 October 2008. Source: SI 2008/2178, r. 26.

In rule 52.3—

(a) in paragraph (4A) omit 'The court may not make such an order in family proceedings.'; and
(b) omit the parenthesis immediately following paragraph (4A).

This amendment is subject to the following transitional provision in SI 2008/2178, r. 44:

The amendments made by rule 26 of these Rules to rule 52.3 do not apply to proceedings where the notice of appeal was filed before 1st October 2008 and rule 52.3 in force immediately before that date will continue to apply to those proceedings as if that rule had not been amended.

PD 52   Practice Direction — Appeals

Amendments (1) to (5) effective from: 1 October 2008. Amendments (6) and (7) effective from: 25 November 2008. Source: 47th Update.

(1) In para. 5.23, for '6.9' substitute '6.28'.
(2) In the table in para. 8.2:
- (a) in the box listing the appeal centres for the Wales Circuit, below 'Swansea' insert 'Mold'; and
- (b) in the box listing the hearing-only centres for the Wales Circuit, insert 'Caernarfon'.
(3) For the heading above para. 15.12, substitute 'Reserved judgments'.
(4) For para. 15.12 substitute:
'15.12 PD 40E contains provisions relating to reserved judgments.'.
(5) Omit paras 15.13 to 15.21.
(6) In the table following para. 20.3, after:
'Representation of the People Act 1983, s. 56 24.4 to 14.6' insert:
'UK Borders Act 2007, s. 11 24.7'.
(7) After para. 24.6 insert:
'*Appeals under section 11 of the UK Borders Act 2007*
24.7
- (1) A person appealing to a county court under the UK Borders Act 2007 ('the Act'), s. 11, against a decision by the Secretary of State to impose a penalty under s. 9(1) of the Act, must, subject to para. (2), file the appellant's notice within 28 days after receiving the penalty notice.
- (2) Where the appellant has given notice of objection to the Secretary of State under s. 10 of the Act within the time prescribed for doing so, the appellant's notice must be filed within 28

days after receiving notice of the Secretary of State's decision in response to the notice of objection.'.

CPR Part 54   Judicial Review and Statutory Review

Amendment effective from: 1 October 2008. Source: SI 2008/2178, r. 27.

In rule 54.28B—

(a) in paragraph (1), for 'rules 6.4(2) and 6.5(5)' substitute 'rules 6.7 and 6.23(2)(a)'; and
(b) in paragraph (2)—
    (i)   in sub-paragraph (a), for 'his' substitute 'the appellant's';
    (ii) in sub-paragraph (b)—
        (aa)   for 'his address' substitute 'the appellant's address'; and
        (bb)   for 'working' substitute 'business'; and
    (iii) at the end of that paragraph, for 'his representative' substitute 'the appellant's representative'.

PD 54   Practice Direction — Judicial Review

Amendment effective from: 1 October 2008. Source: 47th Update.

(1) For para. 6.2 substitute:
    '6.2 Where the defendant or interested party to the claim for judicial review is:
    (a)   the Asylum and Immigration Tribunal, the address for service of the claim form is the Asylum and Immigration Tribunal, Official Correspondence Unit, PO Box 6987, Leicester, LE1 6ZX or fax number (0116) 249 4131;
    (b)   the Crown, service of the claim form must be effected on the solicitor acting for the relevant government department as if the proceedings were civil proceedings as defined in the Crown Proceedings Act 1947.
    (The list published under the Crown Proceedings Act 1947, s. 17, of the solicitors acting in civil proceedings (as defined in that Act) for the different government departments on whom service is to be effected, and of their addresses, [is printed in **appendix 6**].)'.
(2) In para. 18.1(1)(a), for 'Immigration and Nationality Directorate' substitute 'UK Border Agency'.
(3) In para. 18.2:
    (a)   in sub-para. (1)(b)(ii), for 'Immigration and Nationality Directorate's' substitute 'UK Border Agency's'; and
    (b)   in sub-para. (2), for 'Immigration and Nationality Directorate' substitute 'UK Border Agency'.
(4) In the parenthesis below para. 18.2(2):
    (a)   for '6.5(8)' substitute '6.10'; and
    (b)   for 'Immigration and Nationality Directorate' substitute 'UK Border Agency'.

CPR Part 55   Possession Claims

Amendment effective from: 1 October 2008. Source: SI 2008/2178, r. 28.

(a) in rule 55.8(6)—

(i)   for 'he' substitute 'the claimant'; and

(ii) for '6.14(2)(a)' substitute '6.17(2)(a)'; and

(b) in rule 55.23(3), for '6.14(2)(a)' substitute '6.17(2)(a)'.

CPR Part 56   Landlord and Tenant Claims and Miscellaneous Provisions about Land

Amendment effective from: 1 October 2008. Source: SI 2008/2178, r. 29.

(a) in rule 56.1(1)—

    (i)   in sub-paragraph (d) omit 'or';

    (ii) in sub-paragraph (e), for '.' substitute '; or'; and

    (iii) after sub-paragraph (e) insert—

        '(f) section 214 of the Housing Act 2004.';

(b) in rule 56.2(2)—

    (i)   for 'The claim' substitute 'Unless an enactment provides otherwise, the claim'; and

    (ii) for 'his' substitute 'the'; and

(c) in rule 56.3—

    (i)   in paragraph (3)(a)(ii) after ';' insert 'and';

    (ii) omit paragraph (3)(b); and

    (iii) for paragraph (4) substitute—

    '(4) Where the claim is an opposed claim the claimant must use the Part 7 procedure.'.

CPR Part 57   Probate and Inheritance

Amendment effective from: 1 October 2008. Source: SI 2008/2178, r. 30.

(a) in rule 57.4(3)—

    (i)   for '6.19' substitute '6.32 or 6.33';

    (ii) for '6.22' substitute '6.35'; and

    (iii) for 'the practice direction supplementing Section 3 of Part 6' substitute 'Practice Direction B supplementing Part 6'; and

(b) in rule 57.16(4A)—

    (i)   for '6.19' substitute '6.32 or 6.33';

    (ii) for '6.22' substitute '6.35'; and

    (iii) for 'the practice direction supplementing Section III of Part 6' substitute 'Practice Direction B supplementing Part 6'.

CPR Part 58   Commercial Court

Amendment effective from: 1 October 2008. Source: SI 2008/2178, r. 31.

(a) in rule 58.6(3), for 'rules 6.16(4), 6.21(4) and 6.22' substitute 'rules 6.12(3), 6.35 and 6.37(5)'; and

(b) in rule 58.10(2), for 'Rule 6.23 (period' substitute 'Rule 6.35 (in relation to the period'.

PD 58   Practice Direction — Commercial Court

Amendment effective from: 1 October 2008. Source: 47th Update.

(1) In para. 5 of Appendix A to PD 58:
  (a) for 'he' substitute 'that solicitor'; and
  (b) in sub-para. (b):
    (i)   for 'him' substitute 'that person'; and
    (ii) for 'England and Wales' substitute 'the United Kingdom, unless the court orders otherwise'.
(2) In para. (4)(b) of the section headed 'Endorsement' in Appendix A to PD 58:
  (a) for 'him' substitute 'that person'; and
  (b) for 'England and Wales' substitute 'the United Kingdom, unless the court orders otherwise'.

CPR Part 59   Mercantile Courts

Amendment effective from: 1 October 2008. Source: SI 2008/2178, r. 32.

(a) in rule 59.5(3), for '6.16(4), 6.21(4) and 6.22' substitute '6.12(3), 6.35 and 6.37(5)'; and
(b) in rule 59.9(2), for 'Rule 6.23 (period' substitute 'Rule 6.35 (in relation to the period'.

CPR Part 61   Admiralty Claims

Amendment effective from: 1 October 2008. Source: SI 2008/2178, r. 33.

(a) In rule 61.4(7)(b), for 'Section III' substitute 'Section IV'; and
(b) in rule 61.11—
  (i)   in paragraph (5), for 'Section III' substitute 'Section IV'; and
  (ii) in paragraph (7)—
    (aa) in sub-paragraph (a)(ii), for 'he' substitute 'the defendant';
    (bb) in sub-paragraph (b), for 'he' substitute 'the defendant'; and
    (cc) in sub-paragraph (b), for '6.22' substitute '6.35'.

PD 61   Practice Direction — Admiralty Claims

Amendment effective from: 1 October 2008. Source: 47th Update.
In para. 3.6(7), for '6.8' substitute '6.15'.

CPR Part 62   Arbitration Claims

Amendment effective from: 1 October 2008. Source: SI 2008/2178, r. 34.

(a) in rule 62.5(3), for '6.24 to 6.29' substitute '6.40 to 6.46';
(b) in rule 62.16(4), for '6.24 to 6.29' substitute '6.40 to 6.46';

(c) in rule 62.18(8)(b), for '6.24 to 6.29' substitute '6.40 to 6.46'; and
(d) in rule 62.20(1)(a), for 'United Kingdom Overseas Territory (within the meaning of rule 6.18(f))' substitute 'British overseas territory'.

PD 62   Practice Direction — Arbitration

Amendment effective from: 1 October 2008. Source: 47th Update.

(1) In para. 3.1:
    (a) for '6.8' substitute '6.15'; and
    (b) for 'him' substitute 'that party'.
(2) In the parenthesis below para. 3.2, for '6.10' substitute '6.17'.

CPR Part 63   Patents and Other Intellectual Property Claims

Amendment effective from: 1 October 2008. Source: SI 2008/2178, r. 35.

(a) in sub-paragraph (a)—
    (i) for 'Patent' substitute 'Intellectual Property'; and
    (ii) for 'jurisdiction' substitute 'United Kingdom';
(b) in sub-paragraph (b), for '6.19(1) or (1A)' substitute '6.32(1), 6.33(1) or 6.33(2)'; and
(c) in sub-paragraph (b)(i), for 'Patent' substitute 'Intellectual Property'.

CPR Part 65   Proceedings Relating to Anti-social Behaviour and Harassment

Amendment effective from: 1 October 2008. Source: SI 2008/2178, r. 36.

(a) in the table of contents, omit—
    (i) the entry 'VI DRINKING BANNING ORDERS UNDER THE VIOLENT CRIME REDUCTION ACT 2006'; and
    (ii) the entries relating to rules 65.31 to 65.36;
(b) in rule 65.1—
    (i) in paragraph (e), after 'Protection from Harassment Act 1997;' insert 'and'; and
    (ii) omit paragraph (f); and
(c) in rule 65.18(5)—
    (i) for 'he' substitute 'the claimant'; and
    (ii) for '6.14(2)(a)' substitute '6.17(2)(a)'; and
(d) omit Section VI.

PD 65   Practice Direction — Anti-social Behaviour and Harassment

Amendment effective from: 1 October 2008. Source: 47th Update.
Omit Section VI.

PD 66   Practice Direction — Crown Proceedings

Amendment effective from: 1 October 2008. Source: 47th Update.
In para. 2.1, for '6.5(8)' substitute '6.10 or 6.23(7)'.

PD 70   Practice Direction — Enforcement of Judgments and Orders

Amendment effective from: 1 October 2008. Source: 47th Update.
In para. 6A.3:
(a) for 'he' substitute 'that partner or member'; and
(b) in sub-para. (3), for 'Section III' substitute 'Section IV'.

PD 71   Practice Direction — Orders to Obtain Information from Judgment Debtors

Amendment effective from: 1 October 2008. Source: 47th Update.
For para. 3 substitute:
'**Service of Order to Attend Court: Rule 71.3**
3. Service of an order to attend court for questioning may be carried out by:
(a) the judgment creditor (or someone acting on the judgment creditor's behalf);
(b) a High Court enforcement officer; or
(c) a county court bailiff.'.

CPR Part 74   Enforcement of Judgments in Different Jurisdiction

Amendment (a) effective from: 1 October 2008. Amendments (b), (c) and (d) effective 12 December 2008. Source: SI 2008/2178, r. 37.
(a) in rule 74.6—
    (i) in paragraph (1)(a), for 'him' substitute 'the judgment debtor';
    (ii) for paragraph (1)(b) substitute—
        '(b) as provided by—

(i)   section 725 of the Companies Act 1985; or
(ii) the Companies Act 2006; or'; and
(iii) in paragraph (2), for '6.24, 6.25, 6.26 and 6.29' substitute '6.40, 6.42, 6.43 and 6.46';

(b) for rule 74.31(2) and the two parentheses below that rule substitute—
'(2) Where a person applies to enforce an EEO expressed in a foreign currency, the application must contain a certificate of the sterling equivalent of the judgment sum at the close of business on the date nearest preceding the date of the application.

(Part 70 contains further rules about enforcement.)';

(c) in rule 74.32—
(i)   in paragraph (2)(a), after 'order' insert '('the affected persons')';
(ii) in paragraph (2)(b), after 'Wales' insert '('the relevant courts')'; and
(iii) for paragraph (3) substitute—
'(3) Upon service of the order on the affected persons, all enforcement proceedings under the EEO in the relevant courts will cease.'; and

(d) in rule 74.33—
(i)   for the heading to the rule substitute 'Stay of or limitation on enforcement'; and
(ii) in paragraph (1), omit 'by application'.

PD 74B   Practice Direction — European Enforcement Orders

Amendment effective from: 1 October 2008. Source: 47th Update.

(1) In para. 5.2, for 'courts of the member State' substitute 'court'.
(2) For the first sentence in para. 5.3, substitute:
'If judgment is set aside in the court of origin, the judgment creditor must notify all courts in which enforcement proceedings are pending in England and Wales under the EEO as soon as reasonably practicable after the order is served on the judgment creditor.'.
(3) For the heading to para. 6.1 substitute 'An Application for Refusal of Enforcement (Rule 74.32)'.
(4) In para. 6.1, for 'stating' substitute 'showing'.
(5) In para. 6.1(1), after 'irreconcilable' insert 'with the judgment which the judgment creditor is seeking to enforce'.
(6) In para. 7.1, for 'An application must, unless the court orders otherwise,' substitute 'Unless the court orders otherwise, an application must'.
(7) In para. 7.2(2), omit ', including the grounds on which the application is made and the order sought'.
(8) Omit para. 7.3.

PD 77   Practice Direction — Applications for and Relating to Serious Crime Prevention Orders

Amendment effective from: 1 October 2008. Source: 47th Update.

(1) In para. 1.2:
(a) omit 'and' at the end of sub-para. (1);
(b) in sub-para. (2), for 'Act.' substitute 'Act; and'; and
(c) after sub-para. (2) insert:
'(3) include details of any third party whom the applicant believes is likely to be significantly adversely affected by the SCPO and the nature of that adverse effect.'.

(2) In para. 3.1, after sub-para. (2) insert:
  '(2A) where the applicant for the SCPO seeks to vary the SCPO:
    (a) details of any third party whom the applicant believes is likely to be significantly adversely affected by the proposed variation to the SCPO; and
    (b) details of the nature of that adverse effect;'.
(3) In sub-para. (3), for 'person or body other than the applicant for the SCPO' substitute 'third party'.
(4) In sub-para. (4) for 'person or body other than the applicant for the SCPO' substitute 'third party'.

CPR Part 78   European Order for Payment and European Small Claims Procedures

New Part 78 effective from: 12 December 2008 insofar as it relates to European orders for payment under Regulation (EC) No. 1896/2006; 1 January 2009 insofar as it relates to the European small claims procedure under Regulation (EC) No. 861/2007. Source: SI 2008/2178, r. 38 and sch. 2.

78.1 Scope of This Part and Interpretation

(1) Section I contains rules about European orders for payment made under Regulation (EC) No 1896/2006 of the European Parliament and of the Council of 12 December 2006 creating a European order for payment procedure.
(2) Section II contains rules about the European small claims procedure under Regulation (EC) No 861/2007 of the European Parliament and of the Council of 11 July 2007 establishing a European small claims procedure.
(3) In this Part—
    (a) unless otherwise stated, a reference to an Annex is to an Annex to the Practice Direction supplementing this Part; and
    (b) 'Service Regulation' means Regulation (EC) 1393/2007 on service, within the same meaning as rule 6.31(e).
(4) Except where—
    (a) the EOP Regulation (which has the same meaning as in rule 78.2(2)(a));

(b) the ESCP Regulation (which has the same meaning as in rule 78.12(2)(a)); or

(c) the Service Regulation

makes different provisions about the certification or verification of translations, every translation required by this Part or such Regulation must be accompanied by a statement by the person making it that it is a correct translation. The statement must include that person's name, address and qualifications for making the translation.

SECTION I — EUROPEAN ORDER FOR PAYMENT PROCEDURE

78.2 Scope of This Section and Interpretation

(1) This Section applies to applications for European orders for payment and other related proceedings under Regulation (EC) No 1896/2006 of the European Parliament and of the Council of 12 December 2006 creating a European order for payment procedure.

(2) In this Section—

(a) 'EOP Regulation' means Regulation (EC) No 1896/2006 of the European Parliament and of the Council of 12 December 2006 creating a European order for payment procedure. A copy of the EOP Regulation can be found at Annex 1;

(b) 'court of origin' has the meaning given by article 5(4) of the EOP Regulation;

(c) 'EOP' means a European order for payment;

(d) 'EOP application' means an application for an EOP;

(e) 'EOP application form A' means the Application for a European order for payment form A, annexed to the EOP Regulation at Annex I to that Regulation;

(f) 'European order for payment' means an order for payment made by a court under article 12(1) of the EOP Regulation;

(g) 'Member State' has the meaning given by article 2(3) of the EOP Regulation;

(h) 'Member State of origin' has the meaning given by article 5(1) of the EOP Regulation;

(i) 'statement of opposition' means a statement of opposition filed in accordance with article 16 of the EOP Regulation.

EOP Applications Made to a Court in England and Wales

78.3 Application for a European Order for Payment

Where a declaration provided by the claimant under article 7(3) of the EOP Regulation contains any deliberate false statement, rule 32.14 applies as if the EOP application form A were verified by a statement of truth.

(An EOP application is made in accordance with the EOP Regulation and in particular article 7 of that Regulation.)

78.4 Withdrawal of EOP Application

(1) At any stage before a statement of opposition is filed, the claimant may notify the court that the claimant no longer wishes to proceed with the claim.

(2) Where the claimant notifies the court in accordance with paragraph (1)—

(a) the court will notify the defendant that the application has been withdrawn; and

(b) no order as to costs will be made.

78.5 Transfer of Proceedings Where an EOP Application Has Been Opposed

(1) Where a statement of opposition is filed in accordance with article 16 of the EOP Regulation and the claimant has not opposed the transfer of the matter—

(a) the EOP application will be treated as if it had been started as a claim under Part 7 and the EOP application form A will be treated as a Part 7 claim form including particulars of claim; and

(b) thereafter, these Rules apply with necessary modifications and subject to this rule and rules 78.6 and 78.7.

(2) When the court notifies the claimant in accordance with article 17(3) of the EOP Regulation the court will also—

(a) notify the claimant—

     (i) that the EOP application form A is now treated as a Part 7 claim form including particulars of claim; and

     (ii) of the time within which the defendant must respond under rule 78.6; and

  (b) notify the defendant—

     (i) that a statement of opposition has been received;

     (ii) that the application will not continue under Part 78;

     (iii) that the application has been transferred under article 17 of the EOP Regulation;

     (iv) that the EOP application form A is now treated as a Part 7 claim form including particulars of claim; and

     (v) of the time within which the defendant must respond under rule 78.6.

78.6 Filing of Acknowledgment of Service and Defence Where an EOP Application Is Transferred under Article 17 of the EOP Regulation

(1) The defendant must file a defence within 30 days of the date of the notice issued by the court under rule 78.5(2)(b).

(2) If the defendant wishes to dispute the court's jurisdiction, the defendant must instead—

  (a) file an acknowledgment of service within the period specified in paragraph (1); and

  (b) make an application under Part 11 within the period specified in that Part.

(3) Where this rule applies, the following rules do not apply—

  (a) rule 10.1(3);

  (b) rule 10.3; and

  (c) rule 15.4(1).

78.7 Default Judgment

(1) If—

  (a) the defendant fails to file an acknowledgment of service within the period specified in rule 78.6(2)(a); and

  (b) does not within that period—

     (i) file a defence in accordance with Part 15 (except rule 15.4(1)) and rule 78.6(1); or

     (ii) file an admission in accordance with Part 14,

the claimant may obtain default judgment if Part 12 allows it.

(2) Where this rule applies, rule 10.2 does not apply.

78.8 Review in Exceptional Cases

An application for a review under article 20 of the EOP Regulation must be made in accordance with Part 23.

Enforcement of EOPS in England and Wales

78.9 Enforcement of European Orders for Payment

(1) A person seeking to enforce an EOP in England and Wales must file at the court in which enforcement proceedings are to be brought the documents required by article 21 of the EOP Regulation.

(2) Where a person applies to enforce an EOP expressed in a foreign currency, the application must contain a certificate of the sterling equivalent of the judgment sum at the close of business on the date nearest preceding the date of the application.

(Parts 70 to 74 contain further rules about enforcement.)

78.10 Refusal of Enforcement

(1) An application under article 22 of the EOP Regulation that the court should refuse to enforce an EOP must be made in accordance with Part 23 to the court in which the EOP is being enforced.

(2) The judgment debtor must, as soon as practicable, serve copies of any order made under article 22 on—

  (a) all other parties to the proceedings and any other person affected by the order ('the affected persons'); and

(b) any court in which enforcement proceedings of the EOP are pending in England and Wales ('the relevant courts').

(3) Upon service of the order on the affected persons, all enforcement proceedings of the EOP in the relevant courts will cease.

78.11 Stay of or Limitation on Enforcement

(1) Where the defendant has sought a review and also applies for a stay of or limitation on enforcement in accordance with article 23 of the EOP Regulation, such application must be made in accordance with Part 23 to the court in which the EOP is being enforced.

(2) The defendant must, as soon as practicable, serve a copy of any order made under article 23 on—
   (a) all other parties to the proceedings and any other person affected by the order; and
   (b) any court in which enforcement proceedings are pending in England and Wales, and the order will not have effect on any person until it has been served in accordance with this rule and they have received it.

SECTION II — EUROPEAN SMALL CLAIMS PROCEDURE

78.12 Scope of this Section and Interpretation

(1) This Section applies to the European small claims procedure under Regulation (EC) No 861/2007 of the European Parliament and of the Council of 11 July 2007 establishing a European small claims procedure.

(2) In this Section—
   (a) 'ESCP Regulation' means Regulation (EC) No 861/2007 of the European Parliament and of the Council of 11 July 2007 establishing a European small claims procedure. A copy of the ESCP Regulation can be found at Annex 2;
   (b) 'defendant's response' means the response to the ESCP claim form;
   (c) 'ESCP' means the European small claims procedure established by the ESCP Regulation;
   (d) 'ESCP claim form' means the claim form completed and filed in the ESCP;
   (e) 'ESCP counterclaim' has the meaning given to counterclaim by recital 16 of the ESCP Regulation;
   (f) 'ESCP judgment' means a judgment given in the ESCP;
   (g) 'Member State' has the meaning given by article 2(3) of the ESCP Regulation;
   (h) 'Member State of enforcement' is the Member State in which the ESCP judgment is to be enforced;
   (i) 'Member State of judgment' is the Member State in which the ESCP judgment is given.

ESCP Claims Made in a Court in England and Wales

78.13 Filing an ESCP Claim Form

Where a declaration provided by the claimant in the ESCP claim form contains any deliberate false statement, rule 32.14 applies as if the ESCP claim form were verified by a statement of truth.

(An ESCP claim form is completed and filed in accordance with the ESCP Regulation, in particular article 4(1), and in accordance with this paragraph.)

78.14 Allocation of ESCP Claims

(1) ESCP claims are treated as if they were allocated to the small claims track.
(2) Part 27 applies, except rule 27.14.

78.15 Transfer of Proceedings Where the Claim Is Outside the Scope of the ESCP Regulation — Article 4(3) of the ESCP Regulation

(1) Where the court identifies that the claim is outside the scope of the ESCP Regulation, the court will notify the claimant of this in a transfer of proceedings notice.
(2) If the claimant wishes to withdraw the claim, the claimant must notify the court of this within 21 days of the date of the transfer of proceedings notice.
(3) Where the claimant has notified the court in accordance with paragraph (2), the claim is automatically withdrawn.

(4) Where the claimant has not notified the court in accordance with paragraph (2) and the claim is instead to be transferred under article 4(3) of the ESCP Regulation—

    (a) the claim will be treated as if it had been started as a claim under Part 7 and the ESCP claim form will be treated as a Part 7 claim form including particulars of claim; and

    (b) thereafter, these Rules apply with necessary modifications and subject to this rule, and the court will notify the claimant of the transfer and its effect.

78.16 Defendant's Response

Where a declaration provided by the defendant in the defendant's response contains any deliberate false statement, rule 32.14 applies as if the defendant's response were verified by a statement of truth.

(The defendant's response is made in accordance with the ESCP Regulation and in particular article 5(3) of the ESCP Regulation.)

78.17 Transfer of Proceedings Where the Defendant Claims That the Non-Monetary Claim Exceeds the Limit Set in Article 2(1) of the ESCP Regulation — Article 5(5) of the ESCP Regulation

(1) This rule applies where, under article 5(5) of the ESCP Regulation, the defendant claims that the value of a non-monetary claim exceeds the limit in article 2(1) of the ESCP Regulation.

(2) When the court dispatches the defendant's response to the claimant, it will—

    (a) notify the claimant that the court is considering whether the claim is outside the scope of the ESCP Regulation in a consideration of transfer notice; and

    (b) send a copy of the notice to the defendant.

(3) If the claimant wishes to withdraw the claim in the event that the court decides that the claim is outside the scope of the ESCP Regulation the claimant must notify the court and the defendant of this within 21 days of the date of the consideration of transfer notice.

(4) The court will notify the defendant as well as the claimant of its decision whether the claim is outside the scope of the ESCP Regulation.

(Article 5(5) of the ESCP Regulation provides that the court shall decide within 30 days of dispatching the defendant's response to the claimant, whether the claim is within the scope of the ESCP Regulation.)

(5) If the court decides that the claim is outside the scope of the ESCP Regulation and the claimant has notified the court and defendant in accordance with paragraph (3), the claim is automatically withdrawn.

(6) If the court decides that the claim is outside the scope of the ESCP Regulation and the claimant has not notified the court and defendant in accordance with paragraph (3)—

    (a) the claim will be treated as if it had been started as a claim under Part 7 and the ESCP claim form will be treated as a Part 7 claim form including particulars of claim;

    (b) the defendant's response will be treated as a defence; and

    (c) thereafter, these Rules apply with necessary modifications and subject to this rule, and the court will notify the parties.

(7) This rule applies to an ESCP counterclaim as if the counterclaim were an ESCP claim.

78.18 Transfer of Proceedings Where the ESCP Counterclaim Exceeds the Limit Set in Article 2(1) of the ESCP Regulation — Article 5(7) of the ESCP Regulation

(1) Where the ESCP counterclaim exceeds the limit set in article 2(1) of the ESCP Regulation, the court will—

    (a) notify the defendant of this in a transfer of proceedings notice; and

    (b) send a copy of the notice to the claimant,

when the court dispatches the defendant's response to the claimant.

(2) If the defendant wishes to withdraw the ESCP counterclaim, the defendant must notify the court and the claimant of this within 21 days of the date of the transfer of proceedings notice.

(3) If the defendant notifies the court and claimant under paragraph (2), the ESCP counterclaim is automatically withdrawn.

(4) If the defendant does not notify the court and claimant in accordance with paragraph (2)—

(a) the claim will be treated as if it had been started as a claim under Part 7 and the ESCP claim form will be treated as a Part 7 claim form including particulars of claim;

(b) the defendant's response and ESCP counterclaim are to be treated as the defence and counterclaim; and

(c) thereafter, these Rules apply with necessary modifications and subject to this rule, and the court will notify the parties.

78.19 Review of Judgment

An application for a review under article 18 of the ESCP Regulation must be made in accordance with Part 23.

Enforcement of ESCP Judgments in England and Wales

78.20 Enforcement of an ESCP Judgment

(1) A person seeking to enforce an ESCP judgment in England and Wales must file at the court in which enforcement proceedings are to be brought the documents required by article 21 of the ESCP Regulation.

(2) Where a person applies to enforce an ESCP judgment expressed in a foreign currency, the application must contain a certificate of the sterling equivalent of the judgment sum at the close of business on the date nearest preceding the date of the application.

(Parts 70 to 74 contain further rules about enforcement.)

78.21 Refusal of Enforcement

(1) An application under article 22 of the ESCP Regulation that the court should refuse to enforce an ESCP judgment must be made in accordance with Part 23 to the court in which the ESCP judgment is being enforced.

(2) The judgment debtor must, as soon as practicable, serve copies of any order made under article 22 on—

(a) all other parties to the proceedings and any other person affected by the order ('the affected persons'); and

(b) any court in which enforcement proceedings are pending in England and Wales ('the relevant courts').

(3) Upon service of the order on the affected persons, all enforcement proceedings of the ESCP judgment in the relevant courts will cease.

78.22 Stay of or Limitation on Enforcement

(1) An application by the defendant under article 23 of the ESCP Regulation must be made in accordance with Part 23 to the court in which the ESCP judgment is being enforced.

(2) The defendant must, as soon as practicable, serve a copy of any order made under article 23 on—

(a) all other parties to the proceedings and any other person affected by the order; and

(b) any court in which enforcement proceedings are pending in England and Wales,

and the order will not have effect on any person until it has been served in accordance with this rule and they have received it.

PD 78   Practice Direction — European Order for Payment and European Small Claims Procedures

PD 78 comes into force on 12 December 2008 insofar as it relates to the European order for payment; and 1 January 2009 insofar as it relates to the European small claims procedure. Source: 47th Update.

This practice direction supplements CPR, Part 78.

EOP Regulation and Application of the Civil Procedure Rules

1.1 EOP applications are primarily governed by the EOP Regulation. Where the EOP Regulation is silent, the Civil Procedure Rules apply with necessary modifications.

Rule 78.3 Application for a European Order for Payment

2.1 An EOP application form A must be:
  (1) completed in English or accompanied by a translation into English; and
  (2) filed at court in person or by post.
2.2 An EOP application made to the High Court will be assigned to the Queen's Bench Division, but that will not prevent the application being transferred where appropriate.

Filing Documents at Court Other Than the EOP Application Form A

3 Documents other than the EOP application form A that are filed at or sent to the court in the EOP proceedings, including statements of opposition, may be filed, in addition to by post or in person, by:
  (1) fax; or
  (2) other electronic means where the facilities are available.

Service

4 Where the EOP Regulation is silent on service, the Service Regulation and the Civil Procedure Rules apply as appropriate.

Article 9 of the EOP Regulation — Completion or Rectification of the EOP Application Form A

5.1 Article 9 of the EOP Regulation makes provision for the completion or rectification of the EOP application form A within a specified time.
5.2 The time specified for the purposes of art. 9 will normally be within 30 days of the date of the request by the court to complete or rectify the EOP application form A (using form B annexed to the EOP Regulation).

Applications under Part 23

6.1 Where an application is made under Section I of Part 78, there will not normally be an oral hearing.
6.2 Where an oral hearing is to be held, it will normally take place by telephone or video conference.

Rule 78.9 Enforcement of European Orders for Payment

7.1 When an EOP is filed at the High Court or county court in which enforcement proceedings are to be brought, it will be assigned a case number.
7.2 A copy of a document will satisfy the conditions necessary to establish its authenticity if it is an official copy of the court of origin.
7.3 If judgment is set aside in the court of origin, the judgment creditor must notify all courts in which enforcement proceedings are pending in England and Wales under the EOP as soon as reasonably practicable after the order is served on the judgment creditor. Notification may be by any means available including fax, email, post or telephone.

Rule 78.10 An Application for Refusal of Enforcement

8.1 An application must be accompanied by an official copy of the earlier judgment, any other documents relied upon and any translations required by the EOP Regulation.
8.2 Where the applicant relies on art. 22(1) of the EOP Regulation, the application must be supported by written evidence showing:
  (1) why the earlier judgment is irreconcilable with the judgment which the claimant is seeking to enforce; and
  (2) why the irreconcilability was not, and could not have been, raised as an objection in the proceedings in the court of origin.

8.3 Where the applicant relies on art. 22(2), the application must be supported by written evidence of the extent to which the defendant has paid the claimant the amount awarded in the EOP.

Rule 78.11 Stay of or Limitation on Enforcement

9.1 Unless the court orders otherwise, an application must be accompanied by evidence of the review application in the court of origin, including:
(1) the review application or a copy of the review application certified by an appropriate officer of the court of origin; and
(2) where that document is not in English, a translation of it into English.
9.2 The written evidence in support of the application must state:
(1) that a review application has been brought in the member State of origin;
(2) the nature of that review application; and
(3) the date on which the review application was filed, the stage the application has reached and the date by which it is believed that the application will be determined.

ESCP Regulation and Application of the Civil Procedure Rules

10 Claims under the ESCP are primarily governed by the ESCP Regulation. Where the ESCP Regulation is silent, the Civil Procedure Rules apply with necessary modifications. In particular, Part 52 applies to any appeals.

Rule 78.13 Filing an ESCP Claim Form

11 An ESCP claim form must be filed at court in person or by post.

Article 4(4) of the ESCP Regulation — Inadequate or Insufficient Information

12.2 Article 4(4) of the ESCP Regulation makes provision for:
(1) the completion or rectification of the claim form;
(2) the supply of supplementary information or documents; or
(3) the withdrawal of the claim,
within a specified time.
12.2 The time specified for the purposes of art. 4(4) is within 30 days of the date of the request by the court to complete or rectify the claim form (using Form B annexed to the ESCP Regulation).

Rule 78.14 Allocation of ESCP Claims

13.1 Rule 78.14(1) provides that ESCP claims are treated as if they were allocated to the small claims track. However, r. 78.14(2) disapplies r. 27.14 on costs because recital 29 to the ESCP Regulation contains different provisions on costs.

13.2 Rule 26.6(1) (scope of the small claims track) is also disapplied because art. 2(1) of the ESCP Regulation has a different financial limit.

Filing Documents at Court Other Than the ESCP Claim Form

14 Documents other than the ESCP claim form that are filed at or sent to the court in the ESCP proceedings, including the defendant's response, may be filed, in addition to by post or in person, by:
(1) fax; or
(2) other electronic means where the facilities are available.

Service

15 Where the ESCP Regulation is silent on service, the Service Regulation and the Civil Procedure Rules apply as appropriate.

Rule 78.17 Transfer of Proceedings Where the Defendant Claims That the Nonmonetary Claim Exceeds the Limit Set in Article 2(1) of the ESCP Regulation — Article 5(5) of the ESCP Regulation

16.1 Rule 78.17(7) applies to counterclaims as if the counterclaim were an ESCP claim because the second paragraph of art. 5(7) of the ESCP Regulation applies certain provisions about claims in the ESCP Regulation, including art. 5(5), to ESCP counterclaims.

16.2 Attention is also drawn to the first paragraph of art. 5(7) of the ESCP Regulation (transfer of claim and counterclaim in certain circumstances).

Oral Hearing under Article 8 of the ESCP Regulation

17.1 Attention is drawn to art. 5(1) of the ESCP Regulation, which sets out limitations on when oral hearings may be held.

17.2 Where an oral hearing is to be held, it will normally take place by telephone or video conference.

Applications under Part 23

18.1 Where an application is made under Section II of Part 78 there will not normally be an oral hearing.

18.2 Where an oral hearing is to be held, it will normally take place by telephone or video-conference.

Rule 78.20 Enforcement of an ESCP Judgment

19.1 When an ESCP judgment is filed at the High Court or county court in which enforcement proceedings are to be brought, it will be assigned a case number.

19.2 A copy of a document will satisfy the conditions necessary to establish its authenticity if it is an official copy of the courts of the member State of judgment.

19.3 If judgment is set aside in the member State of judgment, the judgment creditor must notify all courts in which proceedings are pending in England and Wales to enforce the ESCP judgment as soon as reasonably practicable after the order is served on the judgment creditor. Notification may be by any means available including fax, email, post or telephone.

Rule 78.21 Application for Refusal of Enforcement

20.1 An application must be accompanied by an official copy of the earlier judgment, any other documents relied upon and any translations required by the ESCP Regulation.

20.2 The application must be supported by written evidence showing:
   (1) why the earlier judgment is irreconcilable with the judgment which the claimant is seeking to enforce; and
   (2) why the irreconcilability was not, and could not have been, raised as an objection in the proceedings in the member State of judgment.

Rule 78.22 Stay of or Limitation on Enforcement – Application Following Application for Review or Where the Judgment Has Been Challenged

21.1 This paragraph applies where a defendant makes an application under art. 23 of the ESCP Regulation in circumstances where:
   (1) an application for review has been made under art. 18 ('review application'); or
   (2) the defendant has challenged the judgment.

21.2 Unless the court orders otherwise, the application under art. 23 must be accompanied by evidence of the review application or challenge in the member State of judgment. This must include a copy of the document initiating the review application or challenge or a copy of the review application or challenge, certified by an appropriate officer of the court in the member State of judgment.

21.3 Where a document is not in English, it must be accompanied by a translation of it into English.

21.4 The written evidence in support of the application must state:
   (1) that a review application or challenge has been brought in the member State of judgment;
   (2) the nature of that review application or challenge; and

(3)   the date on which the review application or challenge was filed, the state of the proceedings and the date by which it is believed that the application or challenge will be determined.

ANNEX 1

THE EOP REGULATION

[Regulation (EC) No. 1896/2006 (the EOP Regulation) may be downloaded from the Eurlex site: <http://eur-lex.europa.eu>]

ANNEX 2

THE ESCP REGULATION

[Regulation (EC) No. 861/2007 (the ESCP Regulation) may be downloaded from the Eurlex site: <http://eur-lex.europa.eu>]

CPR Schedule 1

RSC ORDER 115 — CONFISCATION AND FORFEITURE IN CONNECTION WITH CRIMINAL PROCEEDINGS

Amendment effective from: 1 October 2008. Source: SI 2008/2178, r. 39.
(a)   in rule 17—
    (i)   in paragraph (1)—
        (aa)   for 'delivering it to him' substitute 'delivering it to that person'; and
        (bb)   for 'to him at his' substitute 'to that person's'; and
    (ii)   in paragraph (2), for '6.24, 6.25 and 6.29 shall' substitute '6.40, 6.42 and 6.46'; and
(b)   in rule 33(2), for '6.24, 6.25 and 6.29 shall' substitute '6.40, 6.42 and 6.46'.

CPR Schedule 2

CCR ORDER 27 — ATTACHMENT OF EARNINGS

Amendment effective from: 1 October 2008. Source: SI 2008/2178, r. 40.
(a)   in rule 5(1), for '6.2' substitute '6.20'; and
(b)   in rule 17(3A), for '6.2' substitute '6.20'.

CCR ORDER 28 — JUDGMENT SUMMONSES

Amendment effective from: 1 October 2008. Source: SI 2008/2178, r. 41.
(a)   in rule 2(2)—
    (i)   for 'his' substitute 'the judgment creditor's';
    (ii)   for 'the judgment summons shall' substitute 'the judgment summons will';
    (iii)   omit 'an officer of';
    (iv)   for 'sending it to him' substitute 'sending it to the debtor'; and
    (v)   for 'the date of service shall be' substitute 'the date of service is'; and
(b)   in rule 3—
    (i)   in paragraph (2)—
        (aa)   for 'shall' substitute 'will';
        (bb)   for '6.11' substitute '6.18'; and
        (cc)   omit 'office'; and
    (ii)   in paragraph (3) omit 'shall'.

CCR ORDER 29 — COMMITTAL FOR BREACH OF ORDER OR UNDERTAKING

Amendment effective from: 1 October 2008. Source: SI 2008/2178, r. 42.

In rule 1(6)—
(a) for 'thereof' substitute 'of the judgment or order'; and
(b) in sub-paragraph (b), for 'telegram' substitute 'fax, e-mail'.

CCR ORDER 33 — INTERPLEADER PROCEEDINGS

Amendment effective from: 1 October 2008. Source: SI 2008/2178, r. 43.

In rule 4(3), for '6.2' substitute '6.20'.

Supplement to Appendix 6
Selected Legislation

Supreme Court Act 1981

Amendment effective from: 10 July 2008. Source: Maximum Number of Judges Order 2008 (SI 2008/2178).

In section 2(1) (which specifies the maximum number of ordinary judges of the Court of Appeal) for the words from 'not more' to the end substitute 'not more than 38 ordinary judges.'.

Index